Literate Culture and Tenth-Century Canaan: The Tel Zayit Abecedary in Context

Literate Culture and Tenth-Century Canaan:

The Tel Zayit Abecedary in Context

edited by

Ron E. Tappy and P. Kyle McCarter

To Becky,
With Best Wishes.
Ron E. Tappy

Winona Lake, Indiana

Eisenbrauns

2008

www.eisenbrauns.com

Library of Congress Cataloging-in-Publication Data

Literate culture and tenth-century Canaan : the Tel Zayit abecedary in context / edited by Ron E. Tappy and P. Kyle McCarter.
p. cm.
Includes bibliographical references and indexes.
ISBN 978-1-57506-150-4 (hardback : alk. paper)
1. Tel Zayit abecedary. 2. Inscriptions, Hebrew. 3. Hebrew language–Alphabet. 4. Palestine–Civilization. 5. Excavations (Archaeology)–Israel–Zayit, Tel. I. Tappy, Ron E. II. McCarter, P. Kyle (Peter Kyle), 1945–
PJ5034.9.L58 2008
492.4′11–dc22

2008034695

The paper used in this publication meets the minimum requirements of the American National Standard for Information Sciences – Permanence of Paper for Printed Library Materials, ANSI Z39.48-1984. ⊗™

In Memory of

Mary Ann McCarter
(1914–2007)

Grover Elvin Tappy
(1925–2007)

Contents

Preface ix

Abbreviations xii

Tel Zayit and the Tel Zayit Abecedary in Their Regional Context . . . 1
Ron E. Tappy

Paleographic Notes on the Tel Zayit Abecedary 45
P. Kyle McCarter

The Phoenician Script of the Tel Zayit Abecedary and Putative Evidence for Israelite Literacy 61
Christopher A. Rollston

Writing and Early Iron Age Israel: Before National Scripts, Beyond Nations and States 97
Seth L. Sanders

The Tel Zayit Abecedary in (Social) Context 113
David M. Carr

Indexes 131
Index of Authors 131
Index of Scripture 134
Index of Topics 135

Inside Back Cover: DVD Digital Pictorial Archive of Tel Zayit and the Tel Zayit Abecedary
Bruce Zuckerman, Marilyn J. Lundberg, Zev Radovan, and Ron E. Tappy

Preface

On July 15, the final day of the 2005 excavation season, archaeologists at Tel Zayit, Israel, discovered a heavy limestone boulder that had two unique features: a bowl-shaped hollow had been ground into one side and on the other two lines of writing had been scratched. The special importance of this discovery derives not only from the stone's archaic alphabetic text (a 22-letter abecedary) but also from its well-defined archaeological context – the interior face of a wall belonging to a structure that dates securely to the 10th century B.C.E. and that suffered total destruction by fire sometime in the latter part of that century. In the editio princeps of the Tel Zayit Abecedary, the authors discussed the broader archaeological portrait of the site in the 10th and 9th centuries B.C.E., presented a letter-by-letter paleographic analysis of the inscription, and offered some general observations regarding the historical significance of this discovery.[1]

Much of the extant epigraphic evidence relating to the late Iron I–early Iron II period has come from compromised archaeological contexts, such as the unstratified debris from which the Gezer Calendar was recovered, or has no known provenance data at all, as is true of almost all the inscribed arrowheads from Lebanon. The secure and fully documented context of the discovery of the Tel Zayit Abecedary stands in sharp contrast to this unfortunate situation. The stone's association with a well-preserved destruction level fixes a specific time period within which the conclusions drawn from a paleographic analysis of the inscription itself can be anchored. Together, the archaeological and paleographical data significantly enhance the discussion of the history and material culture of southern Canaan in the 10th century B.C.E.

The Tel Zayit Abecedary represents the linear alphabetic script of the central and southern Canaanite interior at the beginning of the first millennium B.C.E. In the initial publication of the inscription, the authors understood this script to be transitional – that is, to be drawing upon the attributes of the Syro-Phoenician tradition of the early Iron Age while anticipating the distinctive features of the mature Hebrew script of the 9th century and later. In a similarly transitional manner, the site that yielded

1. R. E. Tappy et al., "An Abecedary of the Mid-Tenth Century from the Judaean Shephelah," *BASOR* 344 (2006) 5–46.

the inscription lies in the marginal zone between the hills of ancient Judah to the east and the Philistine coastal plain to the west. The liminal character of both the script and the physical setting of Tel Zayit raises interesting and complex questions that scholars with a variety of expertise and perspective must address together in order to interpret the abecedary. To begin exploring some of the issues involved, we organized and co-chaired a panel held on November 15, 2007, at the annual meeting of the American Schools of Oriental Research in San Diego, California. The contributions to this book grew out of the papers presented by that panel and the formal and informal discussions that followed. Our intent in producing this volume is to encourage discussion of the geographic, paleographic, and cultural contexts of the site and this unique inscription.

To this end we offer five chapters, each containing a contribution by one of the San Diego panelists. In chap. 1, Ron Tappy broadens the archaeological discussion of the site in order to situate Tel Zayit regionally within its historical and (international) political contexts, especially in relation to the emergent Kingdom of Judah. Next (chap. 2) Kyle McCarter offers a paleographical analysis of the script of the abecedary that analyzes its debt to the Old Canaanite tradition of the preceding centuries and to the contemporary script of the Phoenician coast and that assesses its relationship to the Hebrew script of the succeeding period. As part of a wide-ranging discussion of literacy (chap. 3), Christopher Rollston questions the usefulness of abecedaries as markers of scribal education and concludes with a paleographic discussion locating the Tel Zayit script within the Phoenician tradition. In chap. 4, Seth Sanders explores the observation that, in contrast to the texts of contemporary Phoenician and later Iron Age states in the region, the texts of 10th-century Canaan as represented by the Gezer Calendar and the Tel Zayit Abecedary lack any connection to a state bureaucracy or any anticipation of the writing of history. Finally, in chap. 5, David Carr considers the possibility that the existence of a complete abecedary such as the one found at Tel Zayit might point to the emergence of a widespread system of education and scribal training and then broadly examines ways in which the establishment of a scribal culture in ancient Judah might have contributed to the process of state formation.

This collection of essays is not intended to mount a sustained argument in any one direction or to test a single hypothesis. Rather, it aims to promote the discussion of the Tel Zayit Abecedary in particular and the disparate but related issues that pertain to epigraphic discoveries in general.

Our thanks go to Jim Eisenbraun for accepting the proposal for publication of these studies and for providing guidance throughout the publication process. We also acknowledge and thank Connie Gundry Tappy for her dedicated work during the initial editing and preparation of the manuscripts. Without her contribution to this project, the book would never have made it to the publisher on time. Finally, a debt of gratitude goes to Pittsburgh Theological Seminary, the institutional sponsor of The Zeitah Excavations, and to all our private sponsors, especially G. Walter Hansen, who has generously supported this project from its inception.

Ron E. Tappy
P. Kyle McCarter
February 2008

Abbreviations

AASOR	Annual of the American Schools of Oriental Research
AfO	*Archiv für Orientforschung*
AfOB	Archiv für Orientforschung: Beiheft
AOAT	Alter Orient und Altes Testament
AOS	American Oriental Series
ASOR Monographs	American Schools of Oriental Research Monographs
BA	*Biblical Archaeologist*
BAR	*Biblical Archaeology Review*
BASOR	*Bulletin of the American Schools of Oriental Research*
CBQ	*Catholic Biblical Quarterly*
CBQMS	Catholic Biblical Quarterly Monograph Series
ErIsr	*Eretz-Israel*
HSM	Harvard Semitic Monographs
HSS	Harvard Semitic Studies
IEJ	*Israel Exploration Journal*
JBL	*Journal of Biblical Literature*
JCS	*Journal of Cuneiform Studies*
JESHO	*Journal of Economic and Social History of the Orient*
JSOT	*Journal for the Study of the Old Testament*
JSOTSup	Journal for the Study of the Old Testament Supplement Series
OBO	Orbis biblicus et orientalis
OTL	Old Testament Library
PEFQS	Palestine Exploration Fund Quarterly Statement
PEQ	*Palestine Exploration Quarterly*
RB	*Revue biblique*
SAOC	Studies in Ancient Oriental Civilization
SBLDS	Society of Biblical Literature Dissertation Series
SBLRBS	Society of Biblical Literature Resources for Biblical Study
SBLSymS	Society of Biblical Literature Symposium Series
SubBi	Subsidia Biblica
TA	*Tel Aviv*
VT	*Vetus Testamentum*
VTSup	Vetus Testamentum Supplement

Tel Zayit and the Tel Zayit Abecedary in Their Regional Context

RON E. TAPPY
Pittsburgh Theological Seminary

In the Borderlands
You are the battleground
Where enemies are kin to each other;
You are at home, a stranger. . . .
To survive the Borderlands
You must live *sin fronteras*
Be a crossroads.
– *Gloria Anzaldúa, "To Live in the Borderlands Means You"*

The near-30-dunam site of Tel Zayit lies in the strategic Beth Guvrin Valley, roughly halfway between Lachish to the south and Tell eṣ-Ṣâfi to the north (figs. 1–2; see below for further details).[1] Although this area generally belonged to the lowlands district of ancient Judah, it lay in an often-contested zone wherein cultural and certainly political associations might shift from time to time, primarily between the highlands to the east and the coastal plain to the west. In the early Iron Age IIA period, workers placed a heavy limestone boulder in the interior face of a wall belonging to a structure that would suffer total destruction by fire sometime near the close of 10th century B.C.E. The exposed portion of the stone contained two lines of clearly incised letters that make up a 22-character, linear alphabet. The other side of the stone – the part buried within the

1. Since 1999, exploration at the site has proceeded under my direction and the sponsorship of Pittsburgh Theological Seminary. This project is also affiliated with the American Schools of Oriental Research and the W. F. Albright Institute of Archaeological Research. Prior to our fieldwork, this unexcavated site received only meager attention in various informal and more-systematic surveys in the area (see Conder and Kitchener 1883: 258; Aharoni and Amiran 1954: 224 [Hebrew]; *Ḥadashot Archaeologiot* 1979: 31 [Hebrew]; Dagan 1992: 153). For notes on the 19th- to 20th-century C.E. Arab village at Tel Zayit, see also Khalidi 1992: 227.

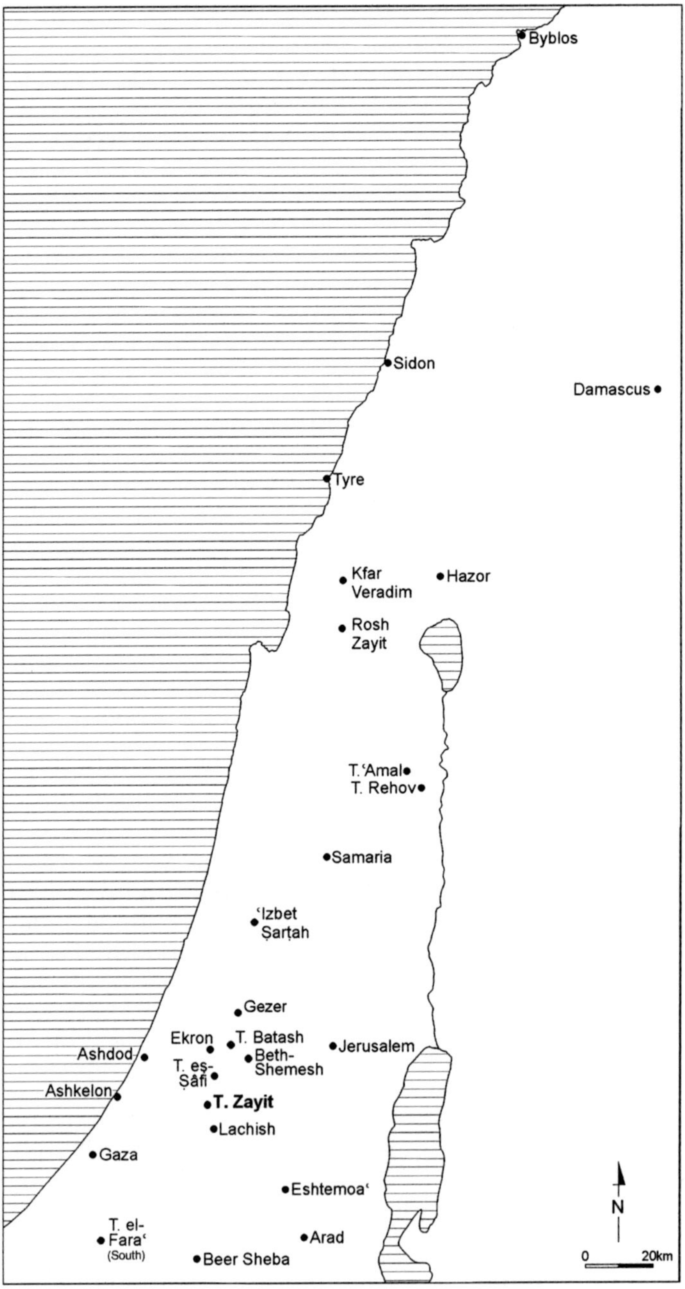

Fig. 1. Map. (J. Rosenberg, Jerusalem)

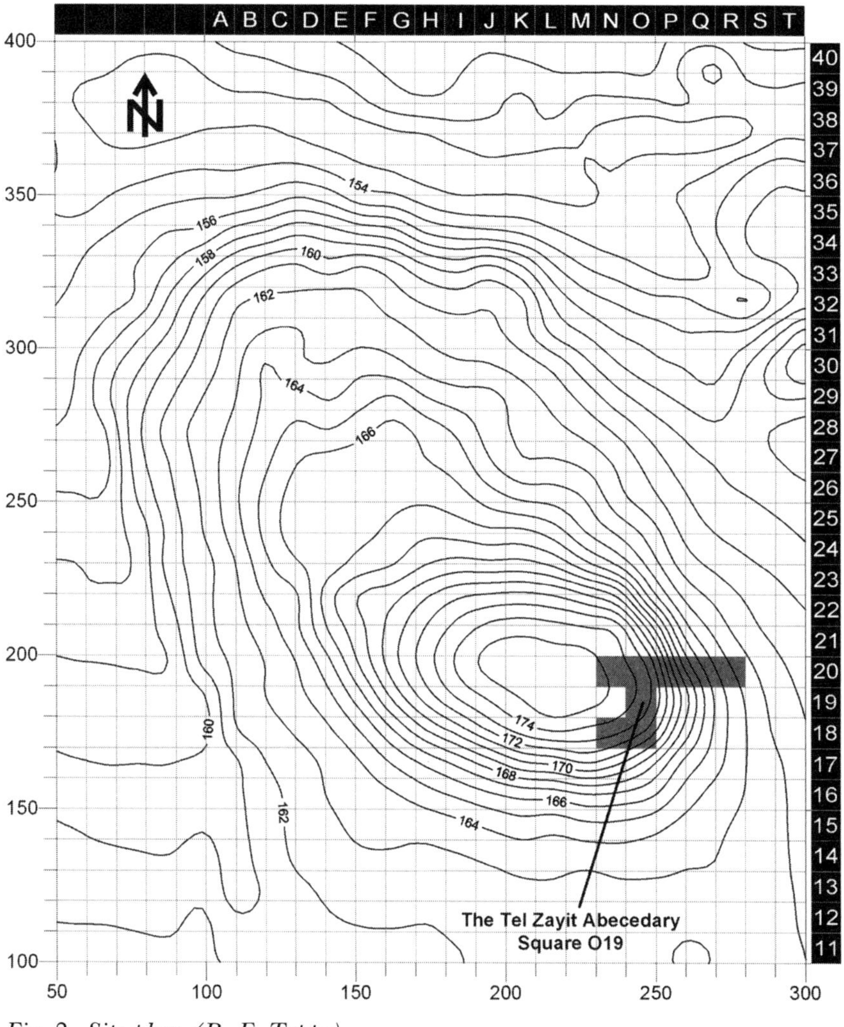

Fig. 2. Site plan. (R. E. Tappy)

makeup of the wall – contained a large, bowl-shaped hollow ground into the central area of the rock (fig. 3a–b).[2] Based on the archaeological exploration of the site thus far, it seems clear that during the functional life

2. For the editio princeps of the Tel Zayit Abecedary, see Tappy et al. 2006. The stone weighs 17.33 kg and measures 37.5 cm × 27 cm × 15.7 cm high. The bowl-shaped hollow opposite the inscribed face of the stone measures 18.5 cm × 14.5 cm × 6.7 cm deep.

of the building that yielded the inscription the ancient town at Tel Zayit maintained its principal affiliations with the inland, highland culture. Following the destruction of the 10th-century structure, several successive deposits sealed the debris and accumulated to a depth of over one meter. These layers include at least two distinct building levels (with the later one showing clear coastal influence and also ending in conflagration) and three related subphases, which together extend from the early 9th to the early 8th century B.C.E.

It seems clear that a scribe put the alphabet on the stone sometime prior to its use in the construction of the 10th-century wall. Thus it is possible that the scribe prepared the inscription for some reason other than the building of this feature and that the excavators, in turn, found the stone in a secondary (or perhaps even tertiary) archaeological context. But whether or not and for how long the inscription served some purpose prior to becoming part of the wall remains difficult to determine. One thing is clear, however: the secure context in which the stone emerged provides a firm terminus ante quem both for the functional life of the building and for the inscription itself. Moreover, because the incising of the stone occurred prior to the construction of the house or building that incorporated it at Tel Zayit, the time of writing likely dates no later than the mid-10th century B.C.E. In other words, the terminus ante quem for the actual engraving of the stone relates directly to the *construction* date (or terminus post quem) of the building, not to the later time of its *destruction*.

Since the early appearance of writing at this moderate-sized, borderland site offers important new evidence for understanding the history of the region during the Iron Age and, more specifically, in the 10th century B.C.E., it is important to situate the culture and politics of the site as precisely as possible within their regional context. Toward this end, I shall compare the depositional history of several key sites in the Shephelah with the deposits at Tel Zayit, outline some important aspects of the location of these sites and offer a specific model by which to interpret them in their broader physical setting, and show the aptness of this model to historical developments in southern Canaan from the 10th through the 7th centuries B.C.E.

Comparison of Deposits

Renewed excavations at Beth-shemesh (see Bunimovitz and Lederman 2001) and the recent, impressive publication of fieldwork at Lachish (Ussishkin 2004) have now yielded a wealth of information that enables us to understand this general region as never before. Because I have addressed elsewhere and in considerable detail the developing circumstances at Lachish during the 10th and 9th centuries B.C.E. (Tappy in press), I need

Fig. 3. Stone with abecedary (above; M. Lundberg and B. Zuckerman, West Semitic Research) and bowl-shaped hollow (below; Zev Radovan, Jerusalem).

only recall that the relative stratigraphic sequences at Lachish and Tel Zayit have refined our understanding of the settlement process in the central and southern Shephelah during a time when the highland culture of Judah claimed substantial settlement and sought to expand its political and economic influence toward its lowlands. Lachish and Tel Zayit claim a similar historical development. Both sites show significant occupations during the Late Bronze Age (with, amazingly, over six vertical meters of remains at Tel Zayit, when the highlands were sparsely settled), occupational gaps throughout most of the Iron Age I period (when hill-country settlements increased dramatically), and renewed occupations sometime during the 10th and 9th centuries B.C.E. (when the founding of hilltop villages accelerated further).

Judging from the latest publication of remains from Lachish, however, it appears that in the 10th century B.C.E. Tel Zayit actually led the way in the settlement of the southern Shephelah – I believe on behalf of the nascent Kingdom of Judah – and that it anticipated by at least half a century the burgeoning occupation of Lachish IVd–a. Admittedly, Tel Zayit appears not to have boasted the monumental architecture and grandeur that came to characterize Lachish; nevertheless, the renewed settlement at Zayit sprang to life already by the early-to-mid-10th century. If the official report from Lachish proves accurate under further scrutiny, then that larger site to the south-southeast of Tel Zayit dominated the lowlands area only in the 9th century, when numerous styles of coastal pottery make their appearance at Tel Zayit.

To the northeast of Tel Zayit, results from the fieldwork at Beth-shemesh have suggested that the process of "state formation in Judah and the organization of the United Monarchy" were well underway there by the last quarter of the 10th century B.C.E. (Bunimovitz and Lederman 2001: 121). In fact, by that time the site boasted an impressive array of monumental features, including a massive fortification system (constructed in approximately the mid-10th century; Bunimovitz and Lederman 2001: 144) that enclosed a large public building in Area B, a huge subterranean water reservoir in Area C, and a so-called commercial zone in Area E (adjacent to a storehouse and large silo).[3] In short, Beth-shemesh was now a substantial, strategic, and vitally important center in the northern Shephelah, and the

3. Admittedly, this conclusion rests primarily on the dating of pottery recovered from construction fills. But the excavators' interpretation results from a painstaking analysis and serious methodological discussion of how best to interpret deposits of this sort. The mere fact that the interpretive process necessitated such detailed work does not make the conclusions wrong, or even questionable. Only the absence of this type of meticulous logic would encourage specious conclusions.

excavators credit this impressive transformation of the city to "a central authority" (Bunimovitz and Lederman 2001: 145) farther up in the mountains, presumably based in Jerusalem.

Beth-shemesh, Tel Zayit, and Lachish, then, have each shed new light on the chronology and cultural history of this important region of the country. By the mid-10th century B.C.E., a new city arose at Beth-shemesh with symbolic architecture and a material culture that reflected an organized political structure in the mountains to the east. This development occurred precisely at the time when the town at Tel Zayit was rebuilt following a 200-year occupational gap during the Iron Age I period, although excavations at Tel Zayit have not yet uncovered the sort of monumental building witnessed at Beth-shemesh (or, later on, at Lachish). The southern and more westerly Shephelah, then, appears to have developed at a more modest pace in the 10th century B.C.E. than did the area controlled by Beth-shemesh slightly farther north. Nevertheless, the settlement at Tel Zayit proves quite significant from a geopolitical standpoint, and the presence there of a mature, 22-letter alphabet attests to this significance.

While both Tel Zayit and Beth-shemesh suffered significant upheavals sometime near the close of the 10th century B.C.E., both towns continued to exist after that time. Lachish, on the other hand, began its new ascent only in the late 10th or (according to Ussishkin) the early to mid-9th century B.C.E. This regional capital soon eclipsed Tel Zayit in both its political and economic value to Judah, but despite "the unusual strength and monumentality of the Level IV fortress city" the principal buildings constructed at Lachish consisted mostly of roughly dressed blocks (not of fine ashlar masonry), homogeneous but moderate quality mud bricks, beams made of local (olive) wood (not cedars from Lebanon), and so on (Ussishkin 2004: 81–82). This royal city, then, emerged gradually over the course of the 9th century and, although it has revealed impressive fortifications (including a city-gate complex) and a centrally located palace that undoubtedly housed a governor or commander appointed from Jerusalem, it did not display the kind of cross-cultural contact (either in materials or techniques) witnessed at other large cities (for example, Gezer, Megiddo, or Dan) or in the central capitals of Jerusalem and Samaria.

The new settlement at Lachish also reveals a "drastic reduction in commercial and cultural connections with the Coastal Plain" throughout the 9th and 8th centuries B.C.E., when the pottery assemblage displays very few coastal forms or traits (Ussishkin 2004: 93). Ussishkin believes that this decline (which contrasts with the situation during the previous occupation of the Late Bronze Age) arose out of the fact that Philistia now "dominated the coastal area, while Judaean Lachish was politically and economically oriented towards Jerusalem" (Ussishkin 2004: 93).

Thus the planning and construction of Lachish Level IV in the 9th century B.C.E. suggest that this city arose as part of a regional project coordinated by Jerusalem and at a time when contemporary changes in the material culture at Tel Zayit indicate a significant transformation in its own political and economic affiliations. With Beth-shemesh established as an anchor of Judean political control in the Sorek Valley, two of the more southerly passageways into the hill country (namely, the Naḥal Guvrin and Naḥal Lachish) aligned themselves in different directions during the course of the 9th century B.C.E. – Lachish toward Jerusalem and Tel Zayit toward the coast. Even during its heyday, Lachish apparently made little or no attempt to broaden its economic ties beyond the boundaries of Judah.[4] At Tel Zayit, on the other hand, an influx of coastal ceramic forms is noticeable rather suddenly in levels dating to the second half of the 9th century B.C.E., the very time during which Lachish established its permanent prominence in this part of the Shephelah on behalf of Judah.

Changes in the strategy promulgated by Jerusalem during the Iron Age IIA period, then, emerge from this brief overview of these three sites. Whereas new developments at Tel Zayit in the Naḥal Guvrin complemented those at Beth-shemesh in the Vale of Sorek in the 10th century B.C.E., both sites (especially Tel Zayit) yielded to the more southerly, stronger, and less exposed site of Lachish beginning in the 9th century B.C.E. (note that virtually all Philistine efforts to penetrate the Shephelah and drive toward the hill country occurred in the more northerly valleys, particularly the Sorek system, and much less often via the Naḥal Lachish [see Tappy in press]). And although Lachish quickly became a royal center, a kind of regional capital, the fact that it did not, according to the excavator, develop fully until around the mid-9th century B.C.E. does not offer a prima facie argument that a centralized political authority could not or did not exist in Jerusalem prior to that time. In fact, excavation results from both Tel Zayit and Beth-shemesh militate against this view.

Bunimovitz and Lederman point to other nearby sites where excavators have attributed clear changes in the archaeological record to "the impact of the United Kingdom" (Bunimovitz and Lederman 2001: 146). For example, they cite Mazar's conclusion that, following the destruction of the Philistine town in Tel Batash (Timnah) Stratum V, the settlement there was only modestly rebuilt during the 10th century B.C.E. In addition, they note the observation drawn by Gitin that the major Philistine center at Tel

4. Not until Level II in the 7th century does the pottery assemblage from Lachish show an appreciable number of coastal-type vessels, but even then not enough data exist to confirm a pattern of clear trade relations between this Judahite city and the coastal region (Ussishkin 2004: 94).

Miqne (Ekron) Stratum IV also declined about the same time as Batash V – that is, around the early-to-mid-10th century B.C.E. – and that the subsequent occupation of this city likewise occurred on a more modest scale in Strata III–II.

Yet, somewhat curiously, while Bunimovitz and Lederman claim that the "impact of the United Kingdom" represents "too general" an explanation for these events, they clearly see this very impact as the impetus behind the concurrent changes toward growth that they describe at Beth-shemesh. Yet it was ultimately, they say, due to the decline of the Philistine threat – not Judahite expansion – in this area "that the young monarchy emerging in the mountain region had to keep a close eye on its periphery. Now was the time to delineate its territory, to consolidate its hold on border communities that might slip away, and to politicise the ethnic entity that would become a nation" (Bunimovitz and Lederman 2001: 147). The increased Philistine presence and threat in the Sorek Valley during the Iron Age I period had created a cultural borderland, a tension zone of sorts, and with the decline of that presence, "the village of Beth-shemesh was turned into a border town in the Sorek Valley with all symbols of centralised political power" (Bunimovitz and Lederman 2001: 147).

The archaeological and historical conclusions of Bunimovitz and Lederman for Tel Beth-shemesh are persuasive. Yet they appear to replace one explanation for the 10th-century rise of Beth-shemesh (the emergent monarchy in the highlands) with another stimulus package (the weakening Philistine presence in the lowlands) without explaining the factors – if different from the first option itself – that led to the second scenario. One might ask why a centralized kingdom in the highlands would have felt the need to shore up its borders (to keep local sites there from "slipping away") at a time when the historical threat in that region was itself disappearing. It seems as though causation would run in the opposite direction: any inland polity would work to protect, strengthen, and even expand its border towns precisely when those places faced the "clear and present danger" of incursion by another, outside political entity. Thus the regression of Philistine pressure in the Sorek Valley (and elsewhere across the Shephelah) simply provided an opportune moment for Judah to attempt its own expansion there.

While the approach of Bunimovitz and Lederman ultimately will not sidestep the debate over the United Monarchy, it should sharpen our methodologies and the questions we ask. In the end, their wise decision to shift the academic discussion from the archaeologically ambiguous capital of Jerusalem to a more anthropological investigation of the border area works only if there existed a viable political entity on each side of that border. One way or the other, the matter returns to the reality or absence of some form of centralized government in the highlands. Because Tel Zayit shares a chronological development with Beth-shemesh but came, within a century of that growth, to stand in a subordinate relationship to Lachish, and because it reveals a somewhat different intrasite character from both of these larger cities, the question arises how best to understand the regional status of these and other nearby locales, both large and small (such as Timnah, Ekron, and Gath to the north of Tel Zayit, and Tell el-ʿAreini and Tell el-Ḥesi to its south), and also how to describe the interregional connections between this constellation of sites and the established political entities lying to the east and west, in Judah and Philistia proper.

A New Model of Intersite Relationships

Understanding better the intersite relationships in and around the Shephelah requires not only an examination of remains from a number of sites but also a new, refined, and more dynamic model against which to evaluate these complex ties. The appearance of a complete abecedary at Tel Zayit surely reflects developments that were occurring in or growing out of other regions in the broader area, such as Phoenicia. Nevertheless, one must interpret this discovery first and foremost within the specific context from which it emerged – in this case, southwestern Canaan, along the Judahite-Philistine border. Generally speaking, this area experienced constant and crucial developments during the Iron Age, from attempts by adjacent bureaucracies to expand their centralized rule (for example, the Philistine Pentapolis on the one hand and Jerusalem on the other) to political and judicial reforms that affected all levels of the local, kinship-based society (for example, the reforms of Jehoshaphat) to a physical destruction, political dismantling, and economic ruination at the close of the 8th century B.C.E. (resulting from Sennacherib's third military campaign, which isolated the Judean hill country through massive military maneuvers along the coast and in the Shephelah [see Tappy 2008]).

Both excavation and regional survey data have shown that Tel Zayit constitutes a borderland site in the western foothills of Judah, lying directly between the highland culture to the east and the coastal culture of the Philistine plain. Tectonic activity and the runoff of water from the eastern mountains resulted in a network of east–west wadis that descend down the seaward slopes of the hill country and through the Shephelah as they approach the inner coastal plain. These drainage systems are, from north to south, the Valley of Ayalon, the Vale of Sorek, Naḥal HaElah, the Valley of Zephatha (= Naḥal Guvrin), Naḥal Lachish, and Wadi el-Ḥesi (modern Naḥal Adorayim, which merges with Naḥal Shiqma just southeast of Tell el-Ḥesi; see fig. 8 below, p. 25).

At least three principal north–south and three east–west roadways through the lowlands of Judah converged near Tel Zayit during various phases of the Iron Age.[5] The longitudinal roads connected Egypt and the northern Sinai Peninsula with the southernmost Philistine capital at Gaza and the lowland area of Judah. Three laterally oriented routes linked coastal centers with the interior hill country by exploiting the natural landscape provided by three of the drainage systems mentioned above: Naḥal HaElah (with a road running from Tell eṣ-Ṣâfi to Azekah and continuing, by way of various routes, to the Judahite highlands between Bethlehem and the Ramah-Mizpah area), Naḥal Guvrin (passing by Tel Zayit, Tel Goded, and Adullam to Khirbet Jedur [biblical Gedor] south of Bethlehem), and Naḥal Lachish (from Ashkelon and its southern flank through the Lachish area and on to the hill country around and south of Hebron). Tel Zayit lies at the western entrance to the central (Naḥal Guvrin) arena.

This convergence of geological and archaeological history correlates well with the outline given in Josh 15:33–44 of the districts and cities belonging to Judah (see Tappy 2000b: 8–11; 2008; in press; Tappy et al. 2006). The author(s) of the Joshua text organized the settlements of the Shephelah, or "lowlands" area, into three geographical groups that follow roughly the Elah (vv. 35–36 = District 2),[6] Lachish (vv. 37–41 = District 3), and Guvrin (vv. 42–44 = District 4) systems (see Rainey 1980; 1983). In each instance, the text appears to identify the natural regime and its political organization by naming a principal (and, in the case of District 4, the westernmost) municipality in the given area before adding a brief list of satellite sites associated with it. The writer names nine towns in the Naḥal Guvrin–District 4 area, with Libnah apparently representing the main city there. These facts are relevant for the ancient identity of Tel Zayit, which undoubtedly relates in some way to the list of sites in the Libnah district (vv. 42–44) and may, in fact, be Libnah itself. If not ancient Libnah, Tel Zayit lay so close to Libnah that it would have followed this important town (even over Lachish) in most regional matters.

In any event, the ancient town of Tel Zayit lay along a topogeographical, geological, cultural, and political interface – at the center of a communication network that connected the highland culture(s) of Judah to the Canaanite and Philistine city-states located near the hilly western

5. See Dorsey 1991: 67–70, with 58, map no. 1; also pp. 189–92, 196 with 182, map no. 13, and 195, map no. 14.

6. From v. 33 through the first site listed in v. 35 (Jarmuth), this roster names eight sites in the Sorek and related valleys before moving to the Naḥal HaElah, for which we read seven sites, with the possible loss of the eighth town, Beth-shemesh, from the roster (Rainey 1983: 7).

flanks, along the Mediterranean seaboard, and toward the principal gateways into Egypt. The site's physical setting raises important issues related to its regional and interregional connections and calls for greater clarification of the interrelationships between this area and those around it. Any information gleaned from a study of this sort will directly bear not only on the overall history of the site but also on the interpretation of the abecedary in particular.

The proposal by Bunimovitz and Lederman to shift the focus of discussion concerning the 10th century from Jerusalem to the Shephelah (the border) is a much welcomed one. It also seems advisable to follow their method further by directing our sights, at least initially, on culture versus politics. That is to say, archaeologists should derive their conclusions first and foremost from the material remains they recover from any number of sites, not from theoretical discussions of this or that possible political system behind the material culture – and certainly not from an a priori or personal bias for or against the political systems. It is in this spirit that I offer the following comments regarding the geographical and political landscape of the Shephelah, and of Tel Zayit in particular, during Iron Age II.

To date, many scholars have used the concepts *core* and *periphery* to illustrate the symbiotic relationship between a cultural or political center and the surrounding territory, however narrowly or broadly defined, in which the center seeks partial or absolute control or influence to promote its self-interests. The concept of periphery, however, proves an inadequate term for describing the cultural history of any one site or the complex relationships between sites in the lowlands of southern Canaan. The term seems to imply an overly specific, discernible line in the sand that marks the outer edge of the center's real or symbolic presence, commercial relations, and more. Although the core-periphery paradigm can sometimes adequately represent various social or cultural realities (such as Fox's [1977] demonstration of ways in which regal-ritual cities recreate themselves in the outlying countryside), it is, more often than not, overly centrist and delimiting. Although this model may symbolize the flow of goods and services to and from the core, it is ultimately centripetal in nature, oriented toward its own center.

Appeals to this model typically seek to show how the two entities (core and periphery) *relate to each other* (as demonstrated in fig. 4). Clearly, an approach of this sort cannot capture the complexities inherent in dealing with multiple cores whose peripheries collide, merge, or overtake one another or form their own local sense of self-identity or definition. Consequently, a more dynamic model is needed to discuss the nature of relationships in situations such as these – that is, relationships between these

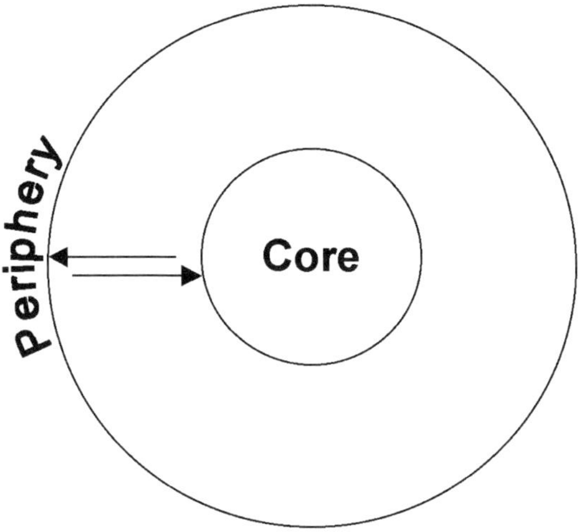

Fig. 4. Core-periphery diagram. (R. E. Tappy)

combined entities (core *and* periphery) and other similar or dissimilar component units around them.

Earlier studies in symbolic anthropology dealing with rituals and rites of passage can help provide a different lens through which to study the archaeology and history of the Shephelah. In perhaps his best-known work – on the rituals associated with transitional stages in human life (work in which he coined the now well-worn phrase "rite of passage") – Arnold van Gennep (1960: 21; originally published in 1908) outlined rite-of-passage rituals as occurring in three discernible phases: *préliminaire*, *liminaire*, and *postliminaire*. Building on van Gennep's threefold structure of separation–transition–reincorporation, Victor Turner (1964; 1967: 93–111; 1969: 94–96, 102–6; 1977) later applied this model to his studies of the Ndembu rituals in northwest Zambia. Turner used the rubrics "separation, margin (*limen*), and aggregation" (V. Turner 1967: 94; see also 1974a; 1985: 158–60) to describe rituals that attend transitions such as males passing from boyhood to manhood, and he focused most of his attention on the *liminaire*, or liminal state of transition.

The typical rite of passage, he said, begins with the separation of the neophyte from his original status and proceeds through a marginal period (*limen*) – wherein "the state of the ritual subject (the 'passenger') is ambiguous" (V. Turner 1967: 94) – before reaching aggregation, that is, the point at which the passage is consummated. Entrance into the limen entails leaving the structural conditions that apply to boys who are not going through the rite of passage and entering a period of unstructured conditions. During the marginal or transitional period, the passenger is neither boy nor man, and the social structures of neither category apply to him; he experiences a period of *interstructural liminality*, of " 'structural invisibility,' ambiguity and neutrality" (V. Turner 1967: 98–99). But, according to Turner, this ambiguous state is not without its benefits. "The liminal group is a community or comity of comrades and not a structure of hierarchically arrayed positions"; that is, the neophytes who are passing through this liminal phase develop a strong sense of comradeship but not as a "brotherhood" or sibling relationship, because these structures entail inherent hierarchy (for example, older brother versus younger). Instead, "complete equality usually characterizes the relationship of neophyte to neophyte" (V. Turner 1967: 100; see also 1974b; 1974c, especially chaps. 5–6; Turner and Turner 1978). Nevertheless, it is during the liminal period and because of their uniform condition that neophytes are most malleable, most passive to their instructors (V. Turner 1967: 101).

I do not wish to apply fully the concept of *communitas* to the situation that existed between Judah and Philistia during the Iron Age.[7] Rather

---

7. Although Turner's work met with immediate acclaim (for sample reviews of V. Turner 1967, see Peacock 1968; Beidelman 1968; and Ben-Amos 1970; for V. Turner 1969 and 1974c, see Graham-White 1975), anthropologists more recently have questioned the degree to which his *communitas* actually constitutes a discernible part of the pilgrimage and liminal state (for example, Sallnow 1981: 177; Eade 2000a: x–xiv; Eade and Sallnow 2000: 3–5). Cohen is certainly correct that "people can participate within the 'same' ritual yet find quite different meanings for it" (1985: 37; see also pp. 55, 71–75). Similarly, neither core nor liminal zone can ever present a totally homogeneous cultural matrix. Thus the frontier residents of ancient Israel undoubtedly often interpreted their changing circumstances differently. (For a particularly strong critique of *communitas* and liminality as a medial step toward "a regenerative return to structure," at least in American culture, see Weber 1995.)

On another point, I would add that in my judgment Turner's identification of the rite of passage as liminal in nature neither neglects nor minimizes the importance of these rituals, nor does it cast them as such extraordinary events that they are outside the realm of daily life. By extension, my application of this concept to the culture and politics in the marginal zone between Judah and Philistia maintains (even highlights) the critical role played by these entities without idealizing either the benefits or hostilities that resulted in the lives of residents there. (A recent collection of essays [Coleman and Eade 2004] includes both critics [see the entries by Coleman, Coleman and Eade, and Mitchell] and proponents [for example, Rosander, Duisch, and Basu] of the Turnerian model; even the critics of than suggesting that the space wherein these two cultures met and competed gave rise to egalitarian structures that evoked a sense of equality among the participants involved, I describe an area that struggled to hold and manage the "co-existence of numerous oppositions" (see Eade 2000b: 52). Any sense of equality among the occupants of a liminal zone develops as much from competition and reciprocity as from conjunction (that is, *communitas*) and is as much a by-product of culture as the disparities that separate antagonistic cores (Sallnow 1981: 177). The marginal zone between ancient Judah and Philistia did not undergo a cultural leveling process at the hands of either core area. In my adaptation of Turner's model of liminality, then, the Shephelah does not represent a structureless area that, for this reason alone, set itself against the highly structured cores that surrounded it. The liminality of the lowlands did not offer the residents there a release from the sociocultural constraints of their respective homelands (see Weber 1995: 528); if anything, the practical expectations and symbolic culture imposed on them by the core areas were designed to highlight their differences.

There is, I believe, much more to gain from (and to critique in) the concepts inherent in the sociological model outlined above. Already, however, the applicability of this approach to a study of borderland towns in the Shephelah becomes apparent (keeping in mind the caveats of n. 11 below). While interstructural liminality maintains a sociological focus in Ndembu rites of passage, this same principle takes on cultural and political aspects for transfrontier towns that lie between and that must function in relation to two or more cores. As "the phenomena and processes of mid-transition" in the Ndembu ritual "paradoxically expose the basic building blocks of culture just when we pass out of and before we re-enter the structural realm" (V. Turner 1967: 110), these towns – such as Tel Zayit – likewise exist betwixt and between the cultural, political, economic, judicial, ideological, theological, and other trappings of the larger, more structured units around them, all of which seek an advantage in the balance of control over the border area.

Towns such as Tel Zayit, then, present somewhat of a paradox in that they may at once constitute some of the core's principal building blocks of political solidarity and also some of the most vulnerable elements in this solidarity. Yet despite their somewhat tenuous status, these cultural borders, with their transfrontier towns and political symbolism, often prove quite durable; they may outlast even significant changes in the official political boundaries of the cultures that surround them (compare the study

Turner acknowledge their great debt to his work [Sallnow 1981: 163–64]; for a solid overview of Turner's life and work, see Deflem 1991.)

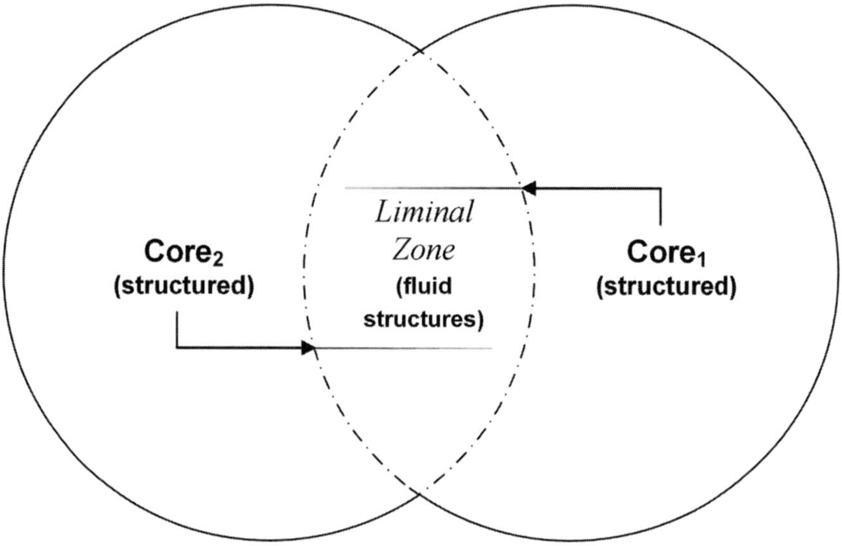

Fig. 5. Liminal zone / Venn diagram. (R. E. Tappy)

of German-speaking St. Felix and Romance-speaking Tret in an alpine valley of northern Italy in Cole and Wolf 1974).[8]

Thus the concept of a limen, or "threshold," characterizes accurately the narrow cultural zones that lie just beyond recognized political boundaries, where competing cores seek to stake their claims through the use of myriad symbols, such as architecture, language, ethnicity, cultural or religious traditions, and so on. Rather than attempting to visualize the complexities inherent in these areas by means of a binary, core-periphery model, a simple Venn diagram proves much more incisive (fig. 5). This diagram portrays situations in which cultural and/or political entities are

8. This reality finds expression in the peripheral zone of the outer Shephelah following Sennacherib's crushing defeat of the region in 701 B.C.E. and his shifting of numerous towns and villages to a new political center. This region maintained its borderland status but with a new and different political orientation; it became a frontier oriented in the opposite direction. While the political status of Tel Zayit and other nearby towns was likely reoriented following Sennacherib's restructuring of the region, it seems unlikely that the day-to-day culture changed to a very large degree. Significant losses to Sennacherib (for example, the sites that suffered massive destruction, such as Lachish) may actually have strengthened to some degree the surviving smaller sites in the region, particularly if these smaller sites were aligned with a new, Assyrian-sponsored center of gravity within the region.

juxtaposed spatially (geographically) to similar entities with which they interact in multiple and varied ways, oftentimes including competition for goods, resources, territory, and control. The diagram works especially well in the analysis of specific sections of borderlines within regions that are naturally, that is, geographically or topographically, delimited (as seen in Sahlins's 1989 and 1998 studies of the Catalan borderlands in the Cerdanya Valley of the Pyrenees Mountains between France and Spain) and for smaller, regional kingdoms that are juxtaposed within a relatively restricted area (such as Judah and Philistia in southern Canaan).

The liminal zone exists along the frontier between two competing cultural or political cores (for which I shall sometimes use the mathematical term *set*). Unlike the periphery, the liminal zone embodies a truly middle and often-contested area that must, by necessity, relate in various ways and at various times to the disparate cultural sets (two or more) that surround it. Rather than representing a cultural or ethnic void, the concept *liminal zone* embodies a place where cultures – through group encounters, positive interactions, and conflict – compete vigorously for presence, meaning, and interpretation. When applied to the Shephelah, the liminal zone represents the theater in which the historical record of relations between the highland cultures to the east and those of the coastal plains to the west played itself out in spatial and temporal terms (compare Wilson and Donnan 1998: 5). In mathematical language, the equation $C_1 \cup C_2$ would represent the union of all aspects of both cores shown in fig. 5, whereas $C_1 \cap C_2$ would reflect only the intersection of their respective symbols and influence and would, therefore, represent their overlap – the liminal zone.

One fact is already apparent: the hybrid character of the liminal-zone concept involves boundaries, borders, and frontiers. Boundaries entail the areas in which the physical and literal structures (that is, cultural norms and symbols) of a particular core remain quite discernible and thereby maintain a substantial identification with this core by promoting or enforcing a range of meanings shared by the inhabitants of this boundary area.[9] The symbols of a cultural or political set are generally clear and understood within the boundaries of the set. Thus a boundary helps to define the outer limits of an established, relatively stable sphere of influence (represented by the broken lines in C_1 and C_2 in fig. 5); it encloses a primary borderland area. Towns along and within the boundary of a particular set will ordinarily display similar traits, thus presenting a coherent definition of the set. The monumental architecture witnessed at Beth-shemesh, therefore, served symbolically to demarcate the boundary of Judah in the Sorek

9. For further discussion of the concept of boundary, see Cohen 1985: 12–15, 39–69.

Valley, and other towns or cities filling the same role in adjacent or nearby locations (such as Lachish in Naḥal Lachish) should display similar features.

A border, on the other hand, represents a relatively narrow area lying just outside the boundary of a particular set. Whereas a boundary conjures the idea of a discernible line, a border typically lies along and just outside this line.[10] It compares to the mat that frames a picture or the ornamental fringe around a rug. As such, it contains the secondary borderlands that attract and prove vital to the self-serving interests of the various cultural sets around it, but its governing influences shift. Because in certain historical periods the border can relate principally to one set or the other, or to more than one set simultaneously, it becomes a true liminal zone (represented by the area *within* the broken lines in fig. 5). The cultural influence (signifying any or all aspects of a society) wielded here by any particular set may occur evenly or sporadically; but, as the arrows in fig. 5 show, this influence is generally stronger near the actual boundaries of the set and diminishes as one moves away from the boundary and through the marginal (liminal) area.[11]

10. See Kavanagh 1994: 75 on the nuances that distinguish "the geographer's boundary" from "the anthropologist's boundary."

11. Because of the richness of meaning that underlies van Gennep's and Turner's term "liminality," I prefer to retain the rubric "liminal zone" in my explanation of the sociologically and culturally complex area squeezed between the two ancient political boundaries of Judah and Philistia. The fact that in more recent cultural research (post-1970s) scholars working in various areas have replaced "liminal" with "border" (see, for example, the feminist studies of Anzaldúa 1987 and the sociological inquiries of Rosaldo 1993) corroborates, in my judgment, the relationship between these concepts that my model seeks to develop. Admittedly, the new cultural anthropologists employ "border" as a means of highlighting the individuality of the actors involved and their resistance to conforming to any dominant culture or established power coordinates. In the term "liminal," they see the latent imperialism of mid-20th-century ethnology. The risk of encountering this pitfall only increases when one attempts to compare an ancient process that was more politically driven (the actions of ancient Judah and Philistia) with more recent ones that are ritually (the Ndembu transition from minority status to adulthood) or sociologically (understanding one's postmodern identity based on race, class, or gender) motivated. Thus, while many nuances embedded in the current (including my own) use of "border" may well apply to individuals or particular towns in the lowlands of southern Canaan, "liminal" continues to capture the needs and desires of the competing cores – the political centers that hoped to expand or at least shore up their rule, indeed, by controlling peripheral space and shaping historical outcomes therein (that is, by acting in imperialistic ways). Ultimately, then, my suggested model for studying the ancient Shephelah incorporates the concepts of

Taken together, the boundary and border of a cultural set constitute the frontier of the unit – space that is inevitably shared with, coveted, and vied for by other, nearby sets.[12] The frontier incorporates not only the area containing a clearly organized and structured cultural or political presence but also the land holding the farthest, dissipating range of this presence. The concept *transfrontier*, then, includes not only the towns that lie along the boundary of a particular cultural or political set but also certain other sites situated beyond that limited space and across the liminal zone itself – that is, sites that in various deliberate ways extend the character of a set into the marginal areas around it. The radius from the core of one cultural area or political entity does not end at a sharp, fixed point; rather, it fades out as the radius from an adjacent core fades in.[13]

Unlike the "periphery," which is conceptually unidirectional (that is, relates primarily to its conceptual counterpart, the core), the liminal zone is bidirectional, and sites within this zone must sort out their affiliations with two or more sometimes cooperative but often opposing cores. Any core can, of course, share liminal zones with more than one adjacent cultural or political unit. Thus in addition to its western front, Judah undoubtedly had to manage similar areas heading in other compass directions, as evident in the back-and-forth maneuvers of Asa of Judah and Baasha of Israel in 1 Kgs 15:16–22. The short distance between Ramah and Mizpah belonged to a rather narrowly defined liminal zone. When compared with the marginal zone in the Shephelah, this zone seems typically to have

---

both local autonomy and centralized power. Interestingly, scholars engaging in the emergent dialogue between science and theology have also found helpful applications for the concept of liminality. Note, for example, the recent work of J. W. van Huyssteen (2006: 1–43, 210), who uses this term when tracing the origin of his own model of *postfoundational rationality* back through the *transversality* of C. Schrag (1994), M. Bakhtin's (1981) idea of the *chronotope* (to express the meeting place of time and space), and, ultimately, to Jean-Paul Sartre's early essays on the transcendence of the ego (1957).

12. On the conflation of the two meanings of region and boundary, see Kopytoff 1987: 9.

13. My definitions of boundary, border, and frontier may differ slightly from the way in which some current "border anthropologists" (who examine relations between modern states) apply these terms. For the border as barrier, see Maravall 1972: 121; Kavanagh 1994; for valuable studies with additional bibliography on the symbolism of borders in establishing national identity, compare Barth 1969; Cohen 1985; 1986; Sahlins 1989; Horsman and Marshall 1994: 41-60, 137-53; Wilson and Donnan 1998. For various other types of identities (for example, household, village, religious, and more), see the essays in Cohen 1986. Note also Anderson 1991.

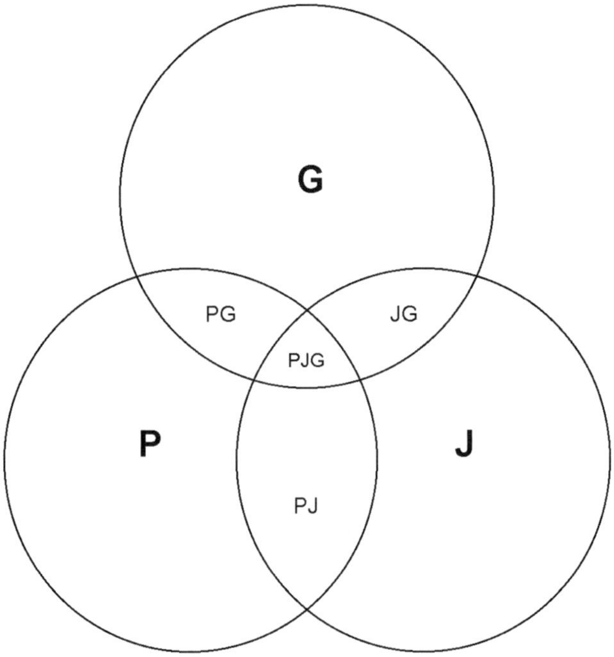

Fig. 6. Complex liminal zone diagram. (R. E. Tappy)

spanned a 3–5-km area beyond the boundaries of the respective political centers of these tightly spaced kingdoms.

For most of these local kingdoms, the complexities of interregional relationships could, and surely did, involve more than one outside set. Thus if a northern set were added to the illustration in fig. 5, regardless of whether it reflected the concerted efforts of Israel as a whole or of a single, powerful city near the borderlands of both Judah and Philistia (such as Gezer), the complexity of relationships would increase dramatically, particularly in the northern Shephelah. Figure 6 shows three hypothetical cores or single sets (J = Judah, P = Philistia, G = Gezer), three double sets (PG, JG, and PJ), and one triple set (PJG) in which all three cores might contend for control and influence. Thus J would have to defend itself and protect its interests against P along one front, against G along another, and – in the most complex intersection – against both P and G. And the same would hold true for the other two primary sets.

In this circumstance, the marginal (or "liminal") zone would experience varying degrees of cultural and political competition and would, therefore, represent a complex liminal zone, even though the groups' impact on the liminal zone may be disproportionate in scale (as indicated in fig. 6 by the somewhat smaller areas of overlapping influence for G). But the circles representing political units that compete within a zone do not function like Borromean Rings, so the withdrawal of one set or cultural core (for example, Gezer) from regional interplay (through, say, a period of internal weakness) would not necessarily imply separation of the others (in this case, Judah and Philistia). On the contrary, each one of the remaining entities would undoubtedly attempt to increase its own presence (both demographically and symbolically) in whatever vacuum might appear in the liminal zone.

In the light of this discussion, any study of borderlands must incorporate the concept of shifting margins between otherwise fairly well-defined entities (see Wilson and Donnan 1998: 8, 13). There always existed an imperfect fit between the tightly spaced, regional kingdoms in Iron Age II Canaan. Regardless of the social criteria along which any core or cultural set develops its self-definition (for example, ethnic, racial, linguistic, cultural, or other forms of homogeneity), "borders always give the lie to this construct" (Horsman and Marshall 1994: 45; see my comments in n. 7 regarding the inability of any core or liminal zone to homogenize fully its local culture[s]). Not only does this approach provide a more realistic model by which to present these Iron Age kingdoms, it also offers significant application to a study of city-state systems such as the one that existed in southern Canaan during the Amarna Age (when Gezer played a more significant role). The inordinate amount of attention that scholars have paid to the urban centers themselves has relegated any consideration of the rich and vital areas between these large entities to second place or, at worst, to oblivion. The question of how ancient polities, whether organized kingdoms or individual city centers, related to one another in the marginal zones between them requires much more concentrated thought in future efforts to understand fully the sociopolitical picture from ancient times.

Two additional observations require attention before we look more directly at the place of Tel Zayit within the liminal zone of the Shephelah. First, no core area or cultural set that manages to establish a presence or some degree of political control in any of the liminal zones around its boundaries can take its foothold for granted. For out of the ethnic, social, cultural, or political continuity that extends beyond the boundaries of adjacent and competing polities can arise a distinct local culture or sense of identity that accepts the maintenance of mobility, various types of interchanges, commercial connections, even kinship ties, and more. This potential can become reality either among the constituent elements within the liminal zone itself or in both (or all) directions away from the zone (through shared connections with surrounding cultural sets that are vying for a place of influence beyond their own boundaries). In other words, "cultures have borders" and "borders have cultures" (as recognized by Rabinowitz 1998: 142; see Barth 1969: 10), and a liminal-zone culture that senses its own autonomy will act accordingly. While the cultural hierarchies and structures of the core stand in a dialectical relationship to the less hierarchical, meshed elements in the liminal zone, the zone itself inevitably develops a cohesive system by which to use its resources, facilitate communications, organize and mobilize people, and so on (see Sallnow 1981: 163).

In certain contexts, therefore, the inhabitants of a liminal zone may well feel torn between the two competing cores that lie beyond their own imagined "borders" and may, as a result, come to feel greater social and demographic unity among themselves if either larger core attempts to impose hard political boundaries within or through their region. Depending on the origin and current status of the many variables (political and military strength, for example) within the liminal zone, locals may view any attempted change as a disruption in their own settled lifestyle or, in more extreme instances, as an overt incursion or even territorial violation by either their own native core or the home core of their neighbors. This phenomenon inherently raises consternation wherever the boundary lines between cultural sets are not rigidly fixed, tenaciously reiterated, and regionally accepted.[14] If this sort of local trend develops over the long haul, it poses a serious concern to all outside, competing cores.

It is not, then, simply the institutional structures (represented, for example, by regional governors) or symbols (embedded, for example, in monumental architecture, writing, and religious or cultic icons) of the core that control the borderland liminal zone. The local customs and will of the people who inhabit these zones play a vital role in the fates of the "outside" cores (see Wilson and Donnan 1998: 24). So while a frontier does not automatically create a new, de facto cultural set, it provides a somewhat unstructured arena (*relative to the surrounding cores*) in which social, cultural, and political processes may evolve with a palatable sense of freedom (see Kopytoff 1987: 14).

Thus, once a viable liminal zone develops, there may arise some degree of dissonance between its local, hybrid culture and the core political systems that sought originally to establish themselves or, in fact, have man-

14. Compare the development of a "local configuration" of Arabesk in the modern province of Hatay, between Turkey and Syria (in Stokes 1998: 283–84); or the independent mindset that sometimes arose in the Cerdanya Valley apart from any larger allegiance to either France or Spain (in Sahlins 1998: 51–52).

aged to maintain some presence in the area (see Wilson 1994: 103–5). Even in the study of much larger, modern political states, "the successful processes of nation and state building may seem to be, in retrospect, a matter of top-down decision making, but in most cases, both historically and in the contemporary world, they are a matter of the dialectics between 'bottom' and 'top', as well as among diverse groups 'at the bottom' " (Donnan and Wilson 1994: 2). As a result, frontiers typically give expression to various motivating forces behind not only cultural transformation (as recognized by F. J. Turner in his 1893 thesis regarding the evolution of American political history [F. J. Turner 1961]) but also behind cultural and historical continuity and conservatism (Kopytoff 1987: 3).

Second, one must always consider the determinative role that geography plays in defining the frontier – that is, the boundaries and liminal zone – of a particular cultural set.[15] Besides helping to delimit interregional boundaries between two or more cultural sets and their shared liminal zone, the natural terrain may also promote various *intra*regional enclaves within the liminal zone itself. The Shephelah region provides a perfect example of this phenomenon, because the lateral valleys that cut down from the Judahite hill country toward the coastal plain help to organize the sites of the lowlands and inner coastal area into recognizable groups (see the discussion of Joshua 15 above).[16] These natural groupings of towns along and within the liminal zone molded to a large extent the economic exchange systems (Tappy in press) and district boundary lines (Tappy 2008) within this area. Moreover, the terrain itself sometimes dictated the field strategy for major military incursions into the liminal area of the Shephelah, as witnessed in the events of Sennacherib's third campaign (again, see Tappy 2008). Tel Zayit itself lies at the mouth of the Guvrin system, near the edge of the inner coastal plain. Unlike the terrain east of the site, the area to the west quickly flattens out and becomes less defined by topographical features (see fig. 7).

Thus, the boundary and liminal zone of a particular core or cultural set embody both the actual territorial frontier and the metaphorical frontier

15. For this aspect with regard to modern states, compare Heslinga 1971 and Wilson 1993; for the Shephelah of ancient Canaan, see Tappy 2008; in press.

16. For example, compare Beth-shemesh and Timnah in the Sorek Valley; Azekah and Gath in the Elah Valley; Tell Judeideh, Tell Bornat, and Tel Zayit in the Guvrin Valley; and Lachish and Tell el-ʿAreini along the Lachish system. Any imposition of artificial boundaries that fails to bear in mind local topography usually generates special concerns in the relationship between a core and its hinterland. Note the discussion in Efrat 1964 of the "Jerusalem Corridor" and the modern use of Beth-shemesh as a regional center.

Fig. 7. Aerial photo of terrain west of Tel Zayit, toward the coast. (Sky View Air Photography, courtesy of R. E. Tappy, The Zeitah Excavations)

that help define, sustain, and give identity to the set (see Wilson and Donnan 1998: 9). Because the liminal zone holds within itself the extremity of a core's extended influence (whether this influence derives its primary meaning from material culture, political institutions, ideological or intellectual history, legal traditions or religious taboos, ethnic or kinship patterns, and/or more), the core can wield considerable, even if spotty, influence in this region. This possibility remains true even though the influence wanes the farther one travels through the zone and away from the sponsoring core. Yet the liminality (represented by a somewhat uneven, shifting, progressively diffuse presence) of the cultural influence, monarchical expansion, or state sovereignty that a core exerts beyond its own recognized boundary does not necessarily imply uniform weakness or evenly increasing subordination to the power of an adjacent cultural set (see Wilson and Donnan 1998: 20). Instead, the successful political exploitation of a liminal zone is designed to offset and overcome just these possibilities; thus, symbolic, fortified centers of one culture often exist very near the boundary of a rival culture.

Historically, geographically, and culturally, the area that lay between an imaginary line running north from ancient Lachish to Beth-shemesh and another that extended from Tell el-Ḥesi through Tell el-ʿAreini and Tel

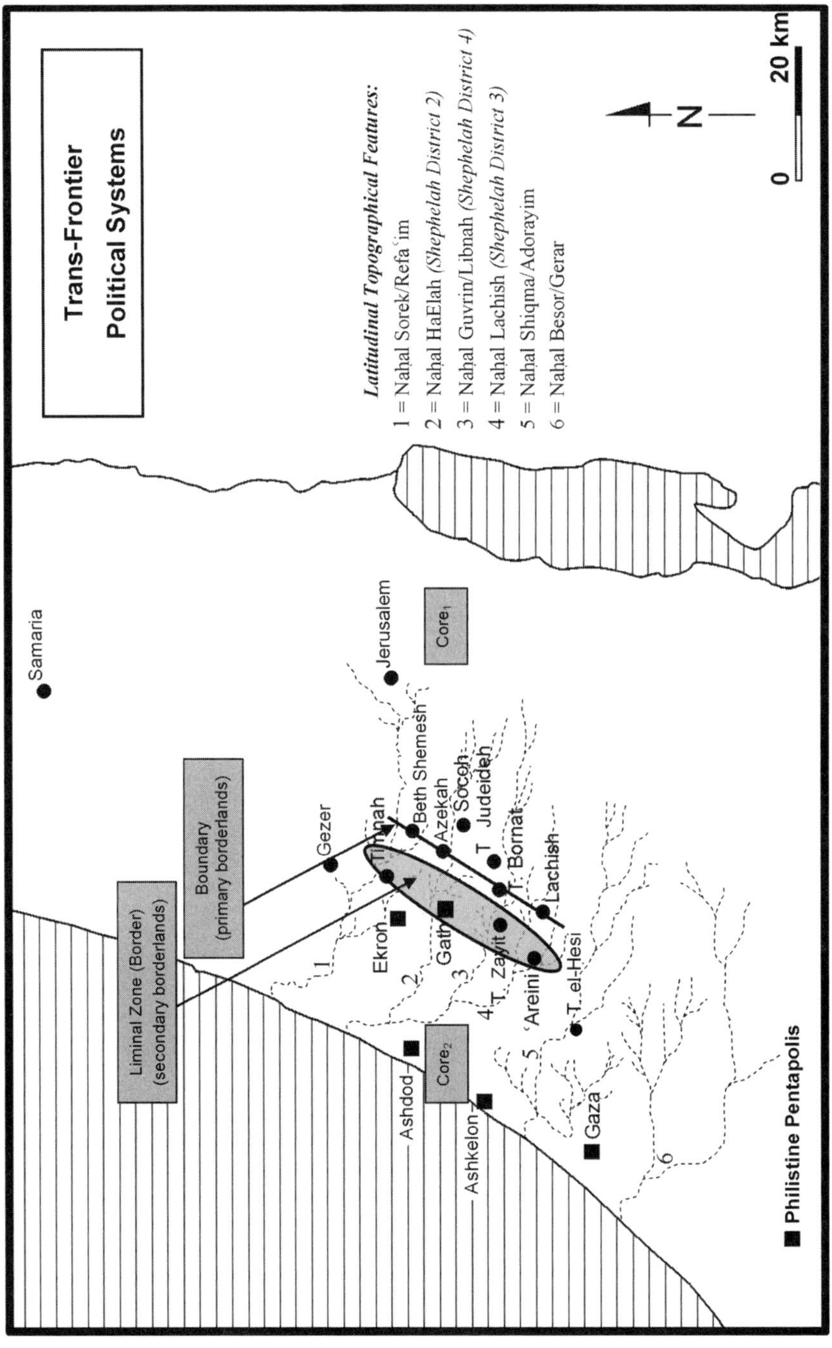

Fig. 8. Map of liminal zone in the Shephelah. (R. E. Tappy)

Zayit to Tel Batash (Timnah), probably taking in at times even Philistine Gath (Tell eṣ-Ṣâfi), provides a perfect example of a limen, or liminal zone, that existed between ancient Judah and Philistia (see fig. 8). To the east of this area, larger, fortified sites such as Beth-shemesh, Azekah, and Lachish (and perhaps the unexcavated Tell Bornat) represent the western boundary of Judah. Each of these sites guards a particular valley passageway into the hill country: Beth-shemesh in the Sorek Valley, Azekah in the Vale of Elah, Tell Bornat in the Naḥal Guvrin, and Lachish in the Naḥal Lachish. At times, other sites such as Tell Judeideh and Socoh undoubtedly served as a backup to these more exposed boundary towns.

Inside (that is, east of) this frontier edge, the cultural and political core/set of the highlands would have experienced greater success at maintaining a more dominant role as arbiter of control and order, judicial organization, cultural and political affairs, kinship structures, and more – that is to say, of all the structured elements that afforded definition to the unit as a whole. In the liminal zone outside the boundary, where the penetration of some of these same elements may have been less structured but still highly symbolic in nature, the arbitration powers of the Judahite core would have grown progressively more limited and challenged, although these powers surely extended beyond the frontier line and some distance through my so-called secondary border area.

Viewed in this light, one should expect to encounter a mix of material culture at Shephelah sites lying along or within the liminal zone – a situation to which the archaeological record bears clear witness. But the mixed elements, whether serving utilitarian or symbolic functions (or both), need not occur uniformly across time and space within this area. By tracking the changes in the material record at selected key sites in the region, both the general history of the area and the specific nature of the liminal zone itself become more apparent.

Applying the Model to the Tenth through Seventh Centuries

Tenth Century B.C.E.

I have already shown that the comparative stratigraphic portraits from Beth-shemesh and Lachish reveal several important points germane to this discussion. For example, based on the current interpretations of the excavators themselves, Judah's Iron Age II interests in the lowlands to its west began in the northern Shephelah during the 10th century B.C.E., when the kingdom fortified Beth-shemesh for both practical and symbolic reasons. By the late 10th or early 9th century – certainly by the mid-9th century – Lachish also became a boundary site representing the highland kingdom and, over the late 9th and 8th centuries B.C.E., assumed its place as the pre-

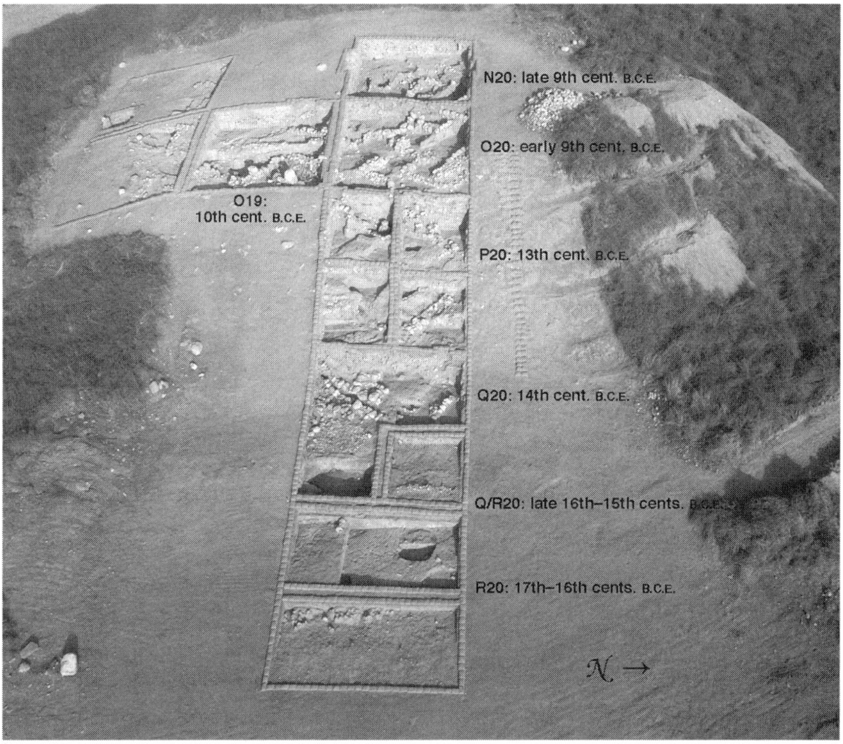

Fig. 9. Aerial photo of Late Bronze / Iron Age excavation areas at Tel Zayit. (Sky View Air Photography, courtesy of R. E. Tappy, The Zeitah Excavations)

miere royal city in the entire region. The line between these two sites represents, in my judgment, the western boundary of Judah in this period. While it is no surprise to find a few signs of coastal contacts in these towns, these elements do not dominate the overall assemblage of artifacts.

In fact, throughout its life in the Iron II period Lachish shows only minimal association with the culture to its west (see n. 4, p. 8 above). Until successive destructions of the site by the Assyrians and Babylonians, the city remained a stronghold of Judah in the southern Shephelah. On the other hand, the fact that archaeologists have assigned the principal Iron II destruction of Beth-shemesh to a variety of causes arises in large measure from the boundary location of the site, near the liminal zone of the Shephelah (suggested causes include [1] a battle between Amaziah and Joash in the early 8th century B.C.E., [2] the capture of the city by the Philistines during the reign of Ahaz in the third quarter of that century, and

[3] the Assyrian military campaign in Philistia and Judah at the close of the period [701 B.C.E.] – the option that now appears to fit the data best).

A short distance to the west of these boundary sites, both Tel Batash and Tel Zayit exhibit marked characteristics of somewhat smaller towns that existed inside the liminal zone between Judah and Philistia. Following an Iron Age I Philistine city that included several building phases in Tel Batash Stratum V, the 10th-century town in Stratum IV appeared, in contrast, to be rather poorly constructed, with open spaces left between buildings and without a major fortification system, although excavators did find a gate area that may have been associated with two solid towers (Mazar and Kelm 1993: 153–54; Mazar and Panitz-Cohen 2001: 154–56, 273–76). The level suffered destruction sometime near the end of the 10th century B.C.E., perhaps during the course of Shishak's march to Kiriath-jearim and Gibeon (Mazar and Kelm 1993: 152, 154; Mazar and Panitz-Cohen 2001: 278–79).

Following the close of the Late Bronze Age at Tel Zayit (with an accumulation of over six vertical meters of occupational levels ranging from Late Bronze Age I through Late Bronze Age IIB; fig. 9), no substantial settlement of the site occurred during the Iron Age I period. Apparently, neither the Philistines nor Judah chose to establish a presence at the erstwhile Late Bronze city. In the 10th century, however, there arose a new town on the summit of the mound. The city's design now featured a series of rooms or buildings with stone walls (one of which held the Tel Zayit Abecedary) or foundations and a combination of flagstone and beaten-earth floors. These chambers incorporated a huge monolith in their design, and they undoubtedly relate to a much larger architectural complex involving at least eight other elements of this sort that are now visible around the eastern, southern, and western shoulders of the tell (see fig. 10a–b).[17]

This beltlike series of houses or small buildings seems comparable to the Stratum XII enclosure at Arad, which dates (now by general consensus) to the prefortress period in the second half of the 10th century B.C.E. As with Tel Batash, the material remains from this stratum generally appear much more modest in both materials and construction compared with the structures at Beth-shemesh. But because the material culture of

17. For a full description of these features and others, see Tappy et al. 2006: 7–22.

Fig. 10 (opposite). (a) Rooms with monolith and (b) volunteers standing on the tops of other exposed monoliths. (The arrow points to the abecedary in Wall 2307/ 2389.) (R. E. Tappy)

both Tel Zayit and Tel Batash reflects the orientation of these towns toward the cultural core in the highlands to the east, we can easily interpret both places as evidence of Judah's attempt to establish its presence farther down in the lowland area just beyond its recognized boundary – that is, in its western liminal zone. Finally, Tel Zayit also suffered a massive destruction by fire late in the 10th century B.C.E. (perhaps at the hands of Shishak, though the historical cause of this destruction remains uncertain).

Ninth Century B.C.E.

At Tel Batash, a hiatus seems to have occurred between the occupations of Stratum IV in the 10th century B.C.E. and Stratum III in the 8th century (Mazar and Panitz-Cohen 2001: 154, 156, 276–77). Fortunately, Tel Zayit now helps to fill this gap and, in doing so, makes an important contribution to our knowledge of the Shephelah during the 9th century, when the political organization of the area underwent significant changes. Lachish now assumed its premiere place among the Judahite sites in the region, even as Tel Zayit fostered increasing connections with the culture(s) of the coastal plain. During the second half of the 9th century B.C.E., it appears (based on preliminary analysis of the pottery assemblage) that coastal ceramic forms dominate the corpus at Tel Zayit. Interestingly, this influence seems to have resulted from peaceful contacts in that direction, contacts perhaps precipitated by Libnah's mid-9th-century revolt against Judah (2 Kgs 8:22 // 2 Chr 21:10) and friendly (economic) overtures from the Philistine cultural core to the west. Whatever lies behind this mutiny, the event reflects – from a Judahite perspective – an appreciable growth in the self-identity and autonomy of a recalcitrant town in the liminal zone. That some of the late-9th-century, coastal-style ceramic forms at Tel Zayit were manufactured locally corroborates this fact even further by perhaps suggesting that at least some coastal potters had taken up residence at the site. For the coastal culture, it meant deeper inroads into the area situated just 7.06 km north and 1.76 km west of Judah's new principal boundary city, Lachish. Thus the changes at Tel Zayit and the rise of Lachish clearly demonstrate a shift in the nature of cultural symbols and political margins in an area between two established cores.

Shortly after this realignment of cultural (and political?) affiliations, Tel Zayit suffered a second destruction by fire, this time in the late 9th-century B.C.E. That the margins in the southern Shephelah had already shifted in favor of the coastal culture strongly suggests that armies from this direction did not precipitate the disaster. Besides, Philistine attempts at eastward expansion always seem to have focused on the Elah and Sorek systems (that is, via the old Judahite District 2 in Joshua 15), not through the more southerly Guvrin or Lachish valley areas (that is, through neither District 4 nor 3; see Tappy et al. 2006: 23 n. 41). If the conflagration does not reflect a retaliation from Judah itself, the perpetrator might well have been Ḥazaʾel of Damascus. Recent excavations at Tell eṣ-Ṣâfi, located 8.09 km to the north-northeast of Tel Zayit, have provided close stratigraphic and ceramic parallels relating to this event. The reduction in or loss of loyalty from Tel Zayit in the second half of the 9th century may also relate in some way to King Jehoshaphat's political and judicial reforms, which had brought with them a strong tendency toward increased centralization in Jerusalem (Tappy 2000a: 332–34). Jehoshaphat's program, perhaps not by accident, coincides with the building of Lachish and the ceding of at least some earlier gains in the liminal zone west of that point.

Eighth Century B.C.E.

Not until the second quarter of the 8th century B.C.E. did a Judahite king (Uzziah) seek to reestablish a stronger presence in this liminal zone (2 Chr 26:6). But the westward military maneuvers that he commissioned focused primarily on northern Philistia and on "breaking into" (not "destroying"; see Japhet 1993: 879 on the verb *prṣ*) the cities of Gath, Jabneh (probably Jabneel, near Ekron; see Josh 15:11), and Ashdod. Uzziah apparently attempted to build "cities in the territory of Ashdod and elsewhere among the Philistines" (see below), while skirting the relatively weak Ekron and avoiding Gaza altogether. Although the biblical description likely embellishes the accomplishment by suggesting actual territorial gains inside Philistia's core, it seems probable that Uzziah did manage some expansion as far west as the lower Sorek Valley (see Mazar 1994: 257).

The strongly fortified settlement at Tel Batash Stratum III belongs to this period of Judahite expansion and continues down to the close of the century. But although at least a dozen LMLK jars and other epigraphic evidence suggest that "the city was ruled by Judah on the eve of Sennacherib's campaign" (Mazar and Kelm 1993: 155; Mazar and Panitz-Cohen 2001: 280), the overall pottery repertoire shows a sharp increase both in the presence and in the specific types of coastal forms (Mazar and Panitz-Cohen 2001: 156–58). This situation may arise from the fact that sometime after Uzziah's successes the Philistines had pushed back against Judah in the northern Shephelah both before and during the reign of King Ahaz.[18] Although the Bible places the oracle in Isa 14:28–32 at the death of Ahaz, the reference to a broken rod that had once smitten the Philistines may reflect

18. See Japhet 1993: 905–6 on the towns from the Sorek Valley and the Valley of Ayalon (Wâdī Selmān) to its north listed in 2 Chr 28:18. This text also claims that the Philistines moved into the Negev of Judah, but none of the cities listed here belong in that region.

a memory of Uzziah (not Ahaz) and of how Philistia had reversed his territorial gains during the time of Ahaz. Once again, a mixing of culture and politics characterizes the liminal zone. But the deep penetration recalled in 2 Chronicles 28 (see n. 18) had, in fact, taken the Philistines through that zone and to or beyond the very boundary of Judah, as evidenced by their aggression east of Timnah as far as Beth-shemesh in the Sorek Valley and their offensive 4 km east of Azekah, to Socoh in the Vale of Elah.

When under Hezekiah Judah later regained enough strength to mount its own intrusion back into this area, the king seems to have concentrated the effort against southern Philistia – in the area east of Gaza. A supplementary record from Sennacherib's 701 B.C.E. campaign, however, may suggest that he also managed to conquer and strengthen Gath (or possibly Ekron; see Tappy 2008: 387–88 n. 35) – the only place-name shared with the biblical account of Uzziah's exploits (cf. Mic 1:10–16). Interestingly, the biblical record remains silent concerning the boundary cities of Beth-shemesh and, east of Azekah, Socoh. But the archaeological record suggests that liminal Timnah had once again fallen under Judahite control by the time of the Assyrian attack in 701 B.C.E. As noted earlier, most of the interplay between the two competing cultures had occurred in the northern valleys – that is, in the Vale of Sorek and Naḥal HaElah. Neither Uzziah nor Hezekiah seems to have focused directly on the area immediately around Tel Zayit in the Naḥal Guvrin (although the archaeological picture remains less clear due to the disturbance of 8th-century levels by later building activities). In any event, it appears that Judah managed to make some gains beyond its western boundary during the course of the 8th century B.C.E. and that even Philistine Gath – if not Ekron itself – suffered under the reality of lying in or near the liminal zone. The overall balance of power within this marginal area between Judah and Philistia, however, had shifted several times over the course of that century – in Judah's favor under Uzziah, toward the Philistines during the reign of Ahaz, and back again to Judah in the time of Hezekiah.

All these interregional, give-and-take affairs were stymied by the complete military domination of the area by the Assyrians during Sennacherib's third campaign. Virtually all of the aforementioned sites endured attacks and suffered either heavy destruction or capture. The topography of the lateral valleys that descend from the highlands through the Shephelah not only provided a basis for Sennacherib's field strategy but also gave shape to the final structure of the Shephelah districts in Josh 15:33–44 (see p. 36 below). Concurrent with the destruction of Lachish Level III, the Assyrians seized numerous (46, according to the Assyrian annals) walled towns or villages and reassigned many of them to rule from the coast. If not before this time, the 8th-century Judahite gains in the liminal zone with Philistia were lost.

Sennacherib quelled the fomenting rebellion by driving a wedge between Judah-Jerusalem and the restless rulers of the coastal plain. The Assyrian strategy focused on renewed subjection of several major cities in Philistia proper, blockading the Judahite capital of Jerusalem, destroying Judah's principal boundary cities, and politically realigning significant portions of the intermediate and strategically crucial Shephelah – the liminal zone. In the years leading up to this invasion, the Philistines had captured Timnah during the reign of Ahaz, only to have Hezekiah subsequently manage to reestablish ties there and to garrison the already fortified city in preparation for Sennacherib's arrival (Mazar and Kelm 1993: 155; Mazar and Panitz-Cohen 2001: 279–81). Perhaps as a reaction to this penetration, the Ekronite noblemen – who had long competed with Judah for control over the Shephelah (cf. Judg 1:18; 1 Sam 5–6, 7:14, 17:52) – deposed their pro-Assyrian ruler (Padi), handed him over to Hezekiah (who then imprisoned him, presumably in Jerusalem [Frahm 1997: 53–54, 59, lines 42–43a; *ARAB* 2 §§240, 311; *ANET* 287; Cogan 2000: 303]), and initiated an anti-Assyrian alliance with the Egyptians/Ethiopians.

The appearance of six LMLK seal impressions at Gath and three others at Ekron (Vaughn 1999: 192–93, nos. 18 and 23) may well reflect Hezekiah's political connections with these subversive actions and his opportunistic incursions into these areas lying a short distance outside Judah's own boundary.[19] Though the status of Gezer (recall fig. 6 above) in this period remains somewhat unclear, the discovery there of additional LMLK seal impressions and unstamped LMLK-type jars may indicate that Hezekiah had also managed to garrison that city sometime shortly before Sennacherib's arrival (see Mazar and Panitz-Cohen 2001: 280–81 n. 3).

In the years prior to 701 B.C.E., Philistine Ekron (Stratum IIA) had expanded slightly as its inhabitants began to resettle the lower city in addition to continuing their use of the elite zone (Gitin 1998: 167 n. 7). But Hezekiah had meddled not only with sites that typically vacillated between Judah and Philistia (Tel Batash [Timnah]) but also with key but more vulnerable Philistine cities that lay within the liminal zone (Tell eṣ-Ṣâfi [Gath]) and even major Philistine centers inside their core or cultural center (Tel Miqne [Ekron] and perhaps even Ashdod). This last aggression, which sought to extend Judah's influence beyond even the long-recognized liminal zone, may well have provided the stimulus for Sennacherib's swift

19. See the so-called Azekah Inscription in Naʾaman 1974: 27, line 11; for interpretive problems surrounding this text, see Tappy 2008: 387–88 n. 35.

response. Ṣidqa, ruler of Ashkelon, also appears to have joined or at least tacitly supported the burgeoning anti-Assyrian alliance, perhaps out of loyalty to longstanding economic connections his port city had held with the lowland and highland towns of Judah (Tappy in press).

This multitiered hierarchy of exchange (which was ultimately controlled by the outlets at coastal ports such as Ashkelon) could not have existed or operated smoothly without the traders and peddlers of the highland culture and market-based middlemen stationed at the transition points in the valleys below. What I have elsewhere called the "fulcrum markets," that is, the towns that lay in the outlying frontier of the inland culture and that helped to regulate the flow of goods from mountains to coast and vice versa, would surely have existed in a state of extreme liminality as they functioned between the two cultural cores. By the late 8th century B.C.E., however, Judah seemed on the edge of upsetting the longstanding, variegated status of sites such as Timnah, Gath, and probably Tel Zayit – a circumstance that won the entire region a violent reaction from Assyria.

Seventh Century B.C.E.

Following this upheaval in the local markets, culture, and politics of the Shephelah, the 7th-century level at Tel Batash (Stratum II) reveals large houses with courtyards, oil presses with crushing basins and extraction vats, stone rollers, and weights, as well as hundreds of restorable vessels from the destruction of this stratum near the close of the 7th century B.C.E. While the pottery assemblage shows both inland and coastal styles, along with some locally made Assyrian imitations, the coastal forms clearly predominate and reveal a striking match to the pottery of Ekron and many similarities to the pottery of Ashdod. It seems clear that this site had become largely coastal in its general cultural and economic affiliations, and the excavator described the overall corpus as "a regional variant of Philistine culture at the end of the Iron Age" (Mazar and Kelm 1993: 156).

Nevertheless, several additional LMLK handles, at least five handles bearing rosette impressions, a Judean pillar figurine, and a series of stone weights point to some degree of continued ties with Judah (Mazar and Panitz-Cohen 2001: 281–82). Within a liminal zone like the lowlands of Judah, there is hardly ever an exclusive presence of one cultural set or the other, as history's pendulum swings slowly toward one core and then back again. Rather, one should expect certain elements to appear from both core areas at any given time in the life of a site, and it then becomes a question of which culture dominates the overall picture. The archaeology of most transfrontier sites in the lowlands of southern Canaan has borne out this general observation. For example, throughout the 9th and 8th centuries B.C.E. the remains from Lachish reveal hardly any cultural or commercial contacts with the coastal area (Ussishkin 2004: 93; see n. 4, p. 8 above). Thus it seems clear that the borderlands (or liminal-zone) town of Timnah now identified primarily with the coastal region, while the boundary city of Lachish maintained its allegiance to Judah. While Timnah's status is certain for the first half of the 7th century, it remains unclear whether King Josiah managed to reestablish Judean control over the town in the latter part of that period (see Mazar and Panitz-Cohen 2001: 282).

As the area slowly recovered from the Assyrian blow to local structures and erstwhile Judahite symbols such as Timnah now served mainly Ekron and Philistia, the biblical writers attempted another cultural ploy – the creation of a literary boundary. The well-known district list for the lowlands of Judah presented in Josh 15:33–44 is followed in vv. 45–47 by the curious inclusion of Ekron, Ashdod, Gaza, and all their towns and villages.

This inclusion raises a tactic that I have not addressed thus far but that constitutes, nonetheless, an integral part of establishing identity and ideology – namely, the use of literary traditions within a core area. As different cultures meet and compete for presence and control in the marginal, liminal zone between them, all aspects of life are brought to bear on the competition when feasible or necessary. The struggle is fought not only through the physical construction of monumental architecture in the outlying sites but also in the popular culture and literary traditions promulgated in the homeland itself.[20] Just as the liminal quality of a border area inherently makes it a tension zone, the day-to-day social interchanges, cultural cooperation, and political negotiations between the actual occupants of that zone simultaneously tend to make the "border" somewhat invisible. The more these interactions are accepted or even promoted at the local level by either side of the border, the more "invisible" the border becomes (see Donnan and Wilson 1994: 6–7; Wilson 1994: 101–3).

When extreme episodes of border disruption further threaten the interests or security of a cultural core, the literary traditions of that group naturally react.[21] A similar literary tactic seems to have unfolded in Judah following Sennacherib's crushing defeat and reorganization of the Shephelah. In the wake of this event, editors altered the old district list from this

20. Compare, for example, Stokes's (1994; 1998) discussion of the role of film, dance, performance, and tabloid reports in the cultural mix of the Hatay province between Turkey and Syria.

21. We see the modern reflex of this phenomenon in governments' use of print and broadcast media during times of war. See Stokes (1994: 41–42) on the value of popular literary representations in gaining visibility for borders.

area (which I take to have originated sometime in the 9th century B.C.E. and to have undergone limited updates thereafter) by including the historically implausible claim that Ekron, Ashdod, and Gaza now constituted official components of the lowland districts of Judah. This literary statement became a cultural symbol for an idealized border zone, a cultural artifice that served as a kind of shorthand notation which conjured up all sorts of recent political, economic, and military history (Tappy 2008).

These same three Philistine cities represent, not coincidentally, the very centers to which Sennacherib gave control over the marginal towns of Judah that he realigned toward the coastal plain (Frahm 1997: 54, 59, line 53; *ARAB* 2 §240; *ANET* 287–88; Cogan 2000: 303). His choice of these particular cities (and not, say, Ashkelon) likely grew out of the longstanding, close connections they had maintained with the Assyrian homeland via the tribute- and wine-bearing envoys they had dispatched to both Nimrud and Nineveh in the decades prior to Sennacherib's third campaign.

The apparent distinction drawn between Ashdod and all other Philistine territories in 2 Chr 26:6b (see above) has garnered significant attention. The passage outlining Uzziah's efforts at expanding Judah's territorial influence (2 Chr 26:6–8) is missing from the books of Kings, and v. 6b in particular presents both grammatical and syntactical difficulties. The notation says only that Uzziah 'built cities *in Ashdod* and among the Philistines' (ויבנה ערים באשדוד ובפלשתים), and to explain the italicized phrase, translators have added the idea that Ashdod itself controlled a certain area surrounding the city ('in *the territory of* Ashdod'). Although a similar assignment of territory to Ashdod may appear in 1 Sam 5:6 (את־אשדוד ואת־גבוליה 'Ashdod and its boundaries/borderlands'), some textual analysts dismiss 2 Chr 26:6b as reflecting only a tendentious expansion by the Chronicler.[22]

Whatever the difficulties in the biblical text, Ashdod may well have competed locally with other Philistine centers for greater sway over the space between them (that is, these cities likely shared their own liminal zones) and also may have played a unique role within the regional strategy of the Assyrians. During the reign of Sargon II, Assyria had subdued the entire Philistine coast in a series of battles spanning nearly a decade and reaching Gaza (and probably also Gibbethon and Ekron) in 720 B.C.E.; Ashdod in 716/715 B.C.E.; and finally Gath (see Younger 2003: 242–43), Ashdod again, and Ashdod's nearby port at Ashdod-yam early in 712 B.C.E.

22. Contrast Ben Zvi 1997: 145–49 with Rainey 1997: 62. Williamson views the second half of this verse as having arisen "secondarily as a confused dittograph" (1982: 334–35). Mazar and Panitz-Cohen (2001: 279–80) correctly note that, given the complex historiographic issues in 1–2 Chronicles, one must evaluate this and other texts of a similar nature against the archaeological data from excavated sites.

At Ashdod itself, the Assyrians constructed a large administrative palace (Sudilovsky 2004), apparently as a base from which to oversee the affairs of the general vicinity. Although Sargon transformed Ashdod and its holdings into an Assyrian province in 712 B.C.E., either he (Galil 1995: 328–29) or, more likely, Sennacherib (Tadmor 1958: 84) later restored the city to its former standing as a tributary kingdom.

Thus not only was the status of towns and villages within the interregional liminal zone changing during and after Sennacherib's invasion but also the rank of certain principal cities within the Philistine core itself. Whatever the official echelon of Ashdod at the time when editors added vv. 45–47 to Joshua 15, their contention that Judah now controlled this area certainly amounted to not only a fictitious claim but also a dangerous claim. All the property touched on in these verses now constituted not just the Philistine core but strategic Assyrian real estate.

Conclusion

Let us return, finally, to Tel Zayit and the abecedary that was discovered there in 2005. This town, which clearly belonged to the liminal zone between ancient Judah and Philistia, helped to open Judah's southwestern frontier already by the mid-10th century B.C.E. Its very existence in this area made an important symbolic statement for the cultural core that lay in the highlands to the east. The presence of an alphabet at Tel Zayit, in my judgment, played a significant role in this symbolism. The contemporaneous monumental architecture at Beth-shemesh served a greater purpose than housing the residents and officials there. Later on, the governor's palace at Lachish and the *absence* of virtually any trace of coastal culture there sent clear messages to the region as a whole. And the 7th-century oil presses at Timnah served a political function that transcended the site's economic ties to Ekron. All these features stood as symbols of different cultural entities that vied for presence in and influence or total control over this area. The Tel Zayit Abecedary also represented at various levels the larger cultural group from which it originated. This situation obtains regardless of which cultural set one sees as the sponsor of the inscription – that is, whether one understands it as a Phoenician script sent from or pointing to a coastal entity, or as an emergent Hebrew script representing the cultural core to the east of Tel Zayit. At this point in the excavations, the archaeology of the level that yielded the stone strongly suggests the latter scenario.

Sometime around the mid-9th century B.C.E., when Tel Zayit – either as biblical Libnah or in connection with Libnah – realigned itself more openly with the cultural horizon from the coast, the principal symbols of Judah shifted slightly south and withdrew to the larger, boundary city of

Lachish. Following those developments, in the first half of the 8th century, Uzziah (and later Hezekiah) focused Judah's expansionistic efforts on the more northerly valleys running down through the Shephelah – that is, on the Sorek and Elah systems where Philistine counterdrives had proven most successful. Together, these kings pushed sundry symbols of their culture as far as Timnah and, at times, even to Philistine Gath and possibly Ekron. During the course of his third campaign, however, Sennacherib disrupted everything in both the liminal zone of the Shephelah and the two cores that straddled it. The regional center at Lachish, which from its inception had displayed firm loyalty to its highland core, suffered massive destruction in 701 B.C.E., and significant tracts of land in the marginal zone immediately west of that site were reassigned from Judahite to neo-Philistine control. Recovery throughout the region proved spotty and protracted and was accomplished only a few decades before the entire area had to face the arrival of Babylon.

Bibliography

Aharoni, Y., and Amiran, R.

1954 A Visit to the Tells of the Shephelah. *Bulletin of the Israel Exploration Society* 224. [Hebrew]

Anderson, B.

1991 *Imagined Communities: Reflections on the Origins and Spread of Nationalism.* Rev. ed. London: Verso.

ANET = Pritchard 1969

Anzaldúa, G.

1987 *Borderlands (La Fontera): The New Mestiza.* San Francisco: Spinsters/Aunt Lute Books.

1996 To Live in the Borderlands Means You. *Frontiers: A Journal of Women Studies* 17/3: 4–5.

ARAB = Luckenbill 1926–27

Bakhtin, M.

1981 *The Dialogic Imagination: Four Essays.* Austin: University of Texas Press.

Barth, F., ed.

1969 *Ethnic Groups and Boundaries: The Social Organization of Cultural Difference.* Boston: Little Brown.

Beidelman, T. O.

1968 Review of *The Forest of Symbols: Aspects of Ndembu Ritual* by Victor Turner. *Africa: Journal of the International African Institute* 38: 483–84.

Ben-Amos, D.

1970 Review of *The Forest of Symbols: Aspects of Ndembu Ritual* by Victor Turner. *Western Folklore* 29: 134–36.

Ben Zvi, E.
1997 The Chronicler as Historian: Building Texts. Pp. 132–49 in *The Chronicler as Historian*, ed. M. P. Graham, K. G. Hoglund, and S. L. McKenzie. JSOTSup 238. Sheffield: Sheffield Academic Press.
Bunimovitz, S., and Lederman, Z.
2001 The Iron Age Fortifications of Tel Beth Shemesh: A 1990–2000 Perspective. *IEJ* 51: 121–47.
Cogan, M.
2000 Sennacherib's Siege of Jerusalem (2.119B). Pp. 302–3 in *The Context of Scripture, Vol. II: Monumental Inscriptions from the Biblical World*, ed. W. W. Hallo and K. L. Younger. Leiden: Brill.
Cohen, A.
1985 *The Symbolic Construction of Community*. London: Ellis Horwood / New York: Tavistock.
Cohen, A., ed.
1986 *Symbolising Boundaries: Identity and Diversity in British Cultures*. Manchester: Manchester University Press.
Cole, J. W., and Wolf, E. R.
1974 *The Hidden Frontier: Ecology and Ethnicity in an Alpine Valley*. London: Academic Press.
Coleman, S., and Eade, J., eds.
2004 *Reframing Pilgrimage: Cultures in Motion*. London: Routledge.
Conder, C. R., and Kitchener, H. H.
1883 *The Survey of Western Palestine: Memoirs of the Topography, Orography, Hydrography, and Archaeology, Volume 3: Judaea*. London: Committee of the Palestine Exploration Fund, 1883. Repr. London: Palestine Exploration Fund.
Dagan, Y.
1992 *The Shephelah during the Period of the Monarchy in Light of Archaeological Excavations and Surveys*. M.A. thesis, Tel Aviv University.
Deflem, M.
1991 Ritual, Anti-Structure, and Religion: A Discussion of Victor Turner's Processual Symbolic Analysis. *Journal for the Scientific Study of Religion* 30/1: 1–25.
Donnan, H., and Wilson, T. M.
1994 An Anthropology of Frontiers. Pp. 1–14 in *Border Approaches: Anthropological Perspectives on Frontiers*, ed. H. Donnan and T. M. Wilson. Lanham, MD: University Press of America.
Eade, J.
2000a Introduction to the Illinois Paperback. Pp. ix–xxvii in *Contesting the Sacred: The Anthropology of Pilgrimage*. Urbana: University of Illinois.
2000b Order and Power at Lourdes: Lay Helpers and the Organization of a Pilgrimage Shrine. Pp. 51–76 in *Contesting the Sacred: The Anthropology of Pilgrimage*. Urbana: University of Illinois.

Eade, J., and Sallnow, M. J., eds.
2000 *Contesting the Sacred: The Anthropology of Pilgrimage.* Urbana: University of Illinois.

Efrat, E.
1964 The Hinterland of the New City of Jerusalem and Its Economic Significance. *Economic Geography* 40: 254–60.

Fox, R. G.
1977 *Urban Anthropology: Cities in Their Cultural Settings.* Englewood Cliffs, NJ: Prentice-Hall.

Frahm, E.
1997 *Einleitung in die Sanherib-Inschriften.* AfOB 26. Vienna: Institut für Orientalistik der Universität Wien.

Galil, G.
1995 A New Look at the 'Azekah Inscription.' *RB* 102: 321–29.

Gennep, A. van
1960 *The Rites of Passage,* trans. M. B. Vizedom and G. L. Caffee. Chicago: University of Chicago Press. [Orig., 1908]

Gitin, S.
1998 Philistia in Transition: The Tenth Century BCE and Beyond. Pp. 162–83 in *Mediterranean Peoples in Transition: Thirteenth to Early Tenth Centuries B.C.E.*, ed. S. Gitin, A. Mazar, and E. Stern. Jerusalem: Israel Exploration Society.

Graham-White, A.
1975 Review of *The Ritual Process: Structure and Anti-Structure* and *Dramas, Fields, and Metaphors: Symbolic Action in Human Society* by Victor Turner. *Educational Theatre Journal* 27: 565–67.

Ḥadashot Archaeologiot
1979 Archaeological News 72: 31. [Hebrew]

Heslinga, M. W.
1971 *The Irish Border as a Cultural Divide: A Contribution to the Study of Regionalism in the British Isles.* Assen: Van Gorcum.

Horsman, M., and Marshall, A.
1994 *After the Nation-State: Citizens, Tribalism and the New World Disorder.* New York: HarperCollins.

Huyssteen, J. W. van
2006 *Alone in the World? Human Uniqueness in Science and Technology.* Grand Rapids: Eerdmans.

Japhet, S.
1993 *I and II Chronicles: A Commentary.* OTL. Louisville: Westminster/John Knox.

Kavanagh, W.
1994 Symbolic Boundaries and 'Real' Borders on the Portuguese–Spanish Frontier. Pp. 75–87 in *Border Approaches: Anthropological Perspectives on Frontiers,* ed. H. Donnan and T. M. Wilson. Lanham, MD: University Press of America.

Khalidi, W., ed.
1992 *All That Remains: The Palestinian Villages Occupied and Depopulated by Israel in 1948*. Washington, DC: Institute for Palestine Studies.

Kopytoff, I.
1987 The Internal African Frontier: The Making of African Political Culture. Pp. 3–84 in *The African Frontier: The Reproduction of Traditional African Societies*, ed. I. Kopytoff. Bloomington: Indiana University Press.

Luckenbill, D. D.
1926–27 *Ancient Records of Assyria and Babylonia*. Vols. 1–2. Chicago: University of Chicago Press.

Maravall, J. A.
1972 *Estado moderno y mentalidad social*. Madrid: Revista de Occidente.

Mazar, A.
1994 The Northern Shephelah in the Iron Age: Some Issues in Biblical History and Archaeology. Pp. 247–67 in *Scripture and Other Artifacts*, ed. M. D. Coogan, J. C. Exum, and L. E. Stager. Louisville: Westminster/John Knox.

Mazar, A., and Kelm, G.
1993 Tel Batash (Timnah). Pp. 152–57 in *The New Encyclopedia of Archaeological Excavations in the Holy Land*, ed. E. Stern. Jerusalem: Israel Exploration Society and Carta.

Mazar, A., and Panitz-Cohen, N.
2001 *Timnah (Tel Batash) II: The Finds from the First Millennium* BCE. Qedem 42. Jerusalem: Institute of Archaeology.

Na'aman, N.
1974 Sennacherib's "Letter to God" on His Campaign to Judah. *BASOR* 214: 25–39.

Peacock, J.
1968 Review of *The Forest of Symbols: Aspects of Ndembu Ritual* by Victor Turner. *American Anthropologist* n.s. 70: 984–85.

Pritchard, J. B.
1969 *Ancient Near Eastern Texts Relating to the Old Testament*. 3rd ed. Princeton, NJ: Princeton University Press.

Rabinowitz, D.
1998 National Identity on the Frontier: Palestinians in the Israeli Education System. Pp. 142–61 in *Border Identities: Nation and State at International Frontiers*, ed. T. M. Wilson and H. Donnan. Cambridge: Cambridge University Press.

Rainey, A. F.
1980 The Administrative Division of the Shephelah. *TA* 7: 194–202.
1983 The Biblical Shephelah of Judah. *BASOR* 251: 1–22.
1997 The Chronicler and His Sources: Historical and Geographical. Pp. 30–72 in *The Chronicler as Historian*, ed. M. P. Graham, K. G. Hoglund, and S. L. McKenzie. JSOTSup 238. Sheffield: Sheffield Academic Press.

Rosaldo, R.
1993 *Culture and Truth: The Remaking of Social Analysis, with a New Introduction.* Boston: Beacon.

Sahlins, P.
1989 *Boundaries: The Making of France and Spain in the Pyrenees.* Berkeley: University of California Press.
1998 State Formation and National Identity in the Catalan Borderlands during the Eighteenth and Nineteenth Centuries. Pp. 31–61 in *Border Identities: Nation and State at International Frontiers,* ed. T. M. Wilson and H. Donnan. Cambridge: Cambridge University Press.

Sallnow, M. J.
1981 Communitas Reconsidered: The Sociology of Andean Pilgrimage. *Man* n.s. 16: 163–82.

Sartre, J.-P.
1957 *The Transcendence of the Ego: An Existentialist Theory of Consciousness,* trans. F. Williams and R. Kirkpatrick. New York: Noonday. [Repr., New York: Hill & Wang, 1989.]

Schrag, C.
1994 Transversal Rationality. Pp. 61–78 in *The Question of Hermeneutics: Essays in Honor of Joseph J. Kockelmans,* ed. T. J. Stapleton. Dordrecht: Kluwer Academic.

Stokes, M.
1994 Local Arabesk, the Hatay and the Turkish–Syrian Border. Pp. 31–51 in *Border Approaches: Anthropological Perspectives on Frontiers,* ed. H. Donnan and T. M. Wilson. Lanham, MD: University Press of America.
1998 Imagining 'the South': Hybridity, Heterotopias and Arabesk on the Turkish-Syrian Border. Pp. 263–88 in *Border Identities: Nation and State at International Frontiers,* ed. T. M. Wilson and H. Donnan. Cambridge: Cambridge University Press.

Sudilovsky, J.
2004 Assyrians in Ashdod: Palace Uncovered Near Israel's Coast. *BAR* 30/6: 12.

Tadmor, H.
1958 The Campaigns of Sargon II of Assur. *JCS* 12: 77–84, 94–96.

Tappy, R. E.
2000a The Code of Kinship in the Ten Commandments. *RB* 107: 321–37.
2000b The 1998 Preliminary Survey of Khirbet Zeitah el Kharab (Tel Zayit) in the Shephelah of Judah. *BASOR* 319: 7–36.
2008 Historical and Geographical Notes on the "Lowland Districts" of Judah in Joshua 15:33–47. *VT* 58: 381–403.
in press East of Ashkelon: The Setting and Settling of the Judaean Lowlands in the Iron Age IIA Period. Forthcoming in a Festschrift in honor of Lawrence E. Stager.

Tappy, R. E.; McCarter, P. K.; Lundberg, M.; and Zuckerman, B.
2006 An Abecedary of the Mid-Tenth Century from the Judaean Shephelah. *BASOR* 344: 5–46.

Turner, F. J.
1961 The Significance of the Frontier in American History. Pp. 28–36 in *Frontier and Section: Selected Essays*, ed. R. A. Billington. Englewood Cliffs, NJ: Prentice-Hall. [Orig., 1893]

Turner, V.
1964 Betwixt and Between: The Liminal Period in *rites de passage*. Pp. 4–20 in *Symposium on New Approaches to the Study of Religion: Proceedings of the 1964 Annual Spring Meeting of the American Ethnological Society*, ed. J. Helm. Seattle: American Ethnological Society.
1967 *The Forest of Symbols: Aspects of Ndembu Ritual.* Ithaca, NY: Cornell University Press.
1969 *The Ritual Process: Structure and Anti-Structure.* Ithaca, NY: Cornell University Press.
1974a Liminal to Liminoid in Play, Flow and Ritual: An Essay in Comparative Symbology. *Rice University Studies* 60: 53–92.
1974b Pilgrimage and Communitas. *Studia Missionalia* 23: 305–27.
1974c *Dramas, Fields and Metaphors: Symbolic Action in Human Society.* Ithaca, NY: Cornell University Press.
1977 Variations on a Theme of Liminality. Pp. 36–52 in *Secular Ritual*, ed. S. F. Moore and B. Myerhoff. Assen: Van Gorcum.
1985 *On the Edge of the Bush: Anthropology as Experience.* Tucson: University of Arizona Press.

Turner, V., and Turner, E.
1978 *Image and Pilgrimage in Christian Culture.* New York: Columbia University Press.

Ussishkin, D.
2004 *The Renewed Archaeological Excavations at Lachish (1973–1994).* 5 vols. Tel Aviv: Emery and Claire Yass Publications in Archaeology of the Institute of Archaeology, Tel Aviv University.

Vaughn, A. G.
1999 *Theology, History, and Archaeology in the Chronicler's Account of Hezekiah.* Archaeology and Biblical Studies 4. Atlanta: Scholars Press.

Weber, D.
1995 From Limen to Border: A Meditation on the Legacy of Victor Turner for American Cultural Studies. *American Quarterly* 47: 525–36.

Williamson, H. G. M.
1982 *1 and 2 Chronicles.* New Century Bible Commentary. Grand Rapids: Eerdmans.

Wilson, T. M.
1993 Frontiers Go but Boundaries Remain: The Irish Border as a Cultural Divide. Pp. 167–87 in *Cultural Change and the New Europe: Perspectives on the European Community*, ed. T. M. Wilson and M. E. Smith. Boulder, CO: Westview.
1994 Symbolic Dimensions to the Irish Border. Pp. 101–18 in *Border Approaches: Anthropological Perspectives on Frontiers*, ed. H. Donnan and T. M. Wilson. Lanham, MD: University Press of America.

Wilson, T. M., and Donnan, H.
1998 Nation, State and Identity at International Borders. Pp. 1–30 in *Border Identities: Nation and State at International Frontiers*, ed. T. M. Wilson and H. Donnan. Cambridge: Cambridge University Press.

Younger, K. L., Jr.
2003 Assyrian Involvement in the Southern Levant at the End of the Eighth Century B.C.E. Pp. 235–63 in *Jerusalem in Bible and Archaeology: The First Temple Period*, ed. A. G. Vaughn and A. E. Killebrew. SBLSymS 18. Atlanta: Society of Biblical Literature.

Paleographic Notes on the Tel Zayit Abecedary

P. KYLE MCCARTER
The Johns Hopkins University

The 2005 discovery at Tel Zayit of an inscribed boulder built into a securely dated 10th-century structure has focused new attention on the status of alphabetic writing in southern Canaan at the beginning of the first millennium B.C.E. Scratched into the surface of the hard limestone is a shallow graffito enumerating the letters of the alphabet. In the *editio princeps* of this abecedary (Tappy et al. 2006), we stressed the importance of the discovery in view of (1) the paucity of other surviving alphabetic remains from the Canaanite interior in the 10th century B.C.E.;[1] and (2) the pivotal position occupied by this period in the history of the alphabet in southern Canaan, when the age of the Old Canaanite scripts of the second millennium was over and the distinctive Hebrew script of the 9th century and later had not yet fully emerged.

The final century of the second millennium B.C.E. witnessed the maturation of alphabetic writing in Syria–Palestine, as the heterogeneity of the Old Canaanite system gradually gave way to standardized scribal practices pertaining to fundamental features such as direction of writing and (with regard to the individual signs) stance. This development is best known

1. Prior to the Tel Zayit discovery, the alphabetic script of the Canaanite interior in the 10th century was known chiefly from the so-called Gezer Calendar (*AHI* 10.001; *HI* 156–65; *KAI* 182; *TSSI* 1: 1–4), a small limestone plaque found in 1908 in Iron II debris. More recent excavations have yielded a scattering of contemporary fragments from a few other sites. These include two short inscriptions from Tel ʿAmal (Tell el-ʿAṣi) west of Beth-shan (Levy and Edelstein 1972: 336, fig. 5 and pl. 25:3, 4 [*HAE* 1: 29–30 and 3: pl. 1.3; *HI* 3]; 340–41 and fig. 18:5); an inscribed rim fragment from Tel Batash in the Judean Shephelah (Kelm and Mazar 1991: 55–56 and fig. 12; 1995: 111, 113 and fig. 6.4; *HAE* 1:30 and 3: pl. 1.4; *HI* 30); an incised gaming board from Beth-shemesh (Bunimovitz and Lederman 1997a: 29; 1997b: 48 [photograph] and 75–76); and an inscribed body sherd from a storage jar found at Reḥov (Mazar 2003: 172–74 and figs. 1–2). See further Tappy et al. 2006: 26–29.

Fig. 1. The Tel Zayit abecedary.

from the well-documented evolution of the script of the Syro-Phoenician bronze arrowheads,[2] the chronology of which spans the 11th century. Early in the arrowhead series, many of the alphabetic signs appear in a variety of forms and – most important for the evolution of the script – in more than one stance, a feature suggestive of the persistence of multi-directional writing.

By the end of the series and the opening of the 10th century, the script had stabilized in a horizontal sinistrograde direction, and the traditional forms and stances of the individual signs had been established. In this final stage, after the process of stabilization was complete, the arrowhead script conformed to the conventions of Linear Phoenician, but the earlier

2. Cross and Milik 1954 [= Cross 2003: 303–8]; Cross 1993 [= Cross 2003: 207–12]. Recently specimens have accumulated rapidly, though not all are likely to be authentic. For updated lists, see Bordreuil 1992; Cross 1996a [= Cross 2003: 195–202]; Deutsch and Heltzer 1997: 9–25; 1999: 13–19; McCarter 1999.

part of the evolution of the arrowhead script is less usefully described as Phoenician than as the last regional development of the Old Canaanite script. This terminology is further supported by the fact that not all the arrowheads come from Phoenicia proper.[3]

This nuanced characterization of the arrowhead script is important to a correct understanding of the 10th-century alphabet of inland Canaan, as represented by the Tel Zayit Abecedary. It is generally acknowledged that Phoenician scribalism had a programmatic effect on the character of alphabetic literacy in the Levant (and beyond) in the early part of the first millennium B.C.E. In the coastal Phoenician script, for example, the Old Canaanite sign inventory was reduced to the 22 necessary to represent the Phoenician consonantal phonemes. Then, when Iron Age scripts emerged as independent traditions in the Levantine interior, each of them employed a 22-letter alphabet regardless of the number of consonantal phonemes the individual languages needed to represent. Indeed, dependence on the Phoenician development seems to be the only way to explain the inconvenient adoption of a 22-letter alphabet by scribes recording these inland dialects. This adoption happened not only in the south with the Hebrew script, which managed its 23 consonantal phonemes with 22 graphemes by the expediency of using a single sign for both *śin* and *šin*, but also in the north with the Old Aramaic script, which represented its 26 consonantal phonemes with the same 22 signs.

Another indication of the influence of Phoenician scribalism on the alphabets of the Syria-Palestinian hinterlands is found in the traditional names of the letters. We might expect the Old Canaanite letter names to be modified in conformity with the standard evolutionary sound changes that occurred during the phonetic development of a language that employed the script, and this modification is evidently what happened in the case of Phoenician. As the Hebrew-Aramaic letter names developed in the interior, however, they included peculiarities that seem best explained by Phoenician influence. The Hebrew-Aramaic letter names *bêt* and *mêm*, for example, arose from original **bayt* and **maym* as the result of glide-sequence or "diphthong" contraction (**ay* → *ê*), which occurred routinely in Phoenician but not in Aramaic or Judahite Hebrew, and the Hebrew-Aramaic letter name *yōd* arose from original **yad* as a consequence of the

3. Unfortunately, almost all of the bronze arrowheads lack archaeological provenance, but anecdotal evidence about their discovery and, more reliably, the internal evidence of their inscriptions suggest that many (perhaps most) come from the Beqaʿ, the site of the Late Bronze Kingdom of Amurru, which persisted into the 11th century. See provisionally the discussion of the arrowhead of Zakarbaʿl, "king of Amurru," in McCarter 1996: 79–80.

so-called Phoenician shift (**á* → *o* in originally open syllables),[4] which is alien to both Hebrew and Aramaic.[5]

If the influence of Phoenician scribalism on the emergent national scripts of first-millennium Syria–Palestine seems clear, however, it does not follow that the alphabet of the 10th-century Canaanite hinterlands can be explained simply as a daughter script of coastal Phoenician. Rather, the inland and coastal scripts are contemporary descendants of a common original. The Tel Zayit Abecedary and the Gezer Calendar are coeval with the sequence of royal Byblian inscriptions, at least in its middle range. More important, alphabetic writing is attested in continuous use in the hinterlands during the period of the emergence of the Phoenician script on the coast. Phoenician culture enjoyed high prestige at the beginning of the first millennium B.C.E., and Phoenician merchants took a leadership role in regional and international trade, so it is not surprising that Phoenician writing influenced inland scribal development. Nevertheless, this influence did not have the character of a parent script expanding into a previously illiterate area.[6]

Indeed, inland Canaan had a long history of alphabetic literacy prior to the 10th century B.C.E. Even if we restrict ourselves to the last three centuries before the turn of the millennium (that is, to the 13th through 11th centuries), we can compile an ample and diverse list of inscribed artifacts recovered from inland sites which, taken together, constitute a substantial corpus of Old Canaanite epigraphic materials that supplement and extend the now extensive corpus of 11th-century arrowheads.[7] This list in-

4. See, for example, Hackett 2004: 371 §3.2.2.

5. In this case, however, there are exceptions (Hebrew-Aramaic letter names that escaped Phoenician influence) including uncontracted *záyin* and *ʿáyin*, which preserve original **zayn* and **ʿayn* (compare *záyin* to Greek *zēta*, which suggests Phoenician **zên* or **zêt*, unless the Greek letter name arose from pattern leveling in recitation [*zēta, ēta, thēta*]). This phenomenon suggests a pattern of dialectic mixing in the Hebrew-Aramaic letter names. Note, however, that the list of exceptions should not include *waw* and *taw*, which did not arise from primitive glide sequences (*waw* ← **waww-* [cf. Greek *fau*] and *taw* ← **taww-* [cf. Greek *tau*]).

6. In the words of Cross (1979: 108 n. 48; 2003: 339–40 n. 51), "Earlier Proto-Canaanite was in use in Palestine, and the shift to Linear Phoenician was a matter of following fashion rather than taking up alphabetic writing for the first time." Rather than a "shift to Linear Phoenician" in Palestine, I should prefer to speak of a regional script development profoundly influenced by Linear Phoenician.

7. The arrowheads themselves may be included in the list because of the likely provenance of many of them in the interior Lebanese valley, as noted above. Not included, however, are contemporary items found at coastal sites, such as the Ṣarepta dipinto of the late 13th century (Pritchard 1975: 101 and fig. 55.1) or the

cludes, from the 13th century, Lachish bowl no. 1, the Lachish ewer, and the Lachish ostracon;[8] from the late 13th and early 12th centuries, the Raddana jar handle, the Qubūr Walaydah inscription, the Beth-shemesh ostracon, and the Tell eṣ-Ṣārem (Reḥov) sherd;[9] from the second half of the 12th century, the ʿIzbet Ṣarṭah ostracon; and from the 11th century, in addition to the bronze arrowheads, the Revadim (ʾAbbaʾ) seal, and the Manaḥat sherd.[10]

Seen in the context of this list of archaic epigraphs from inland Canaanite sites of the last three centuries of the second millennium, the paleographic character of the script of the 10th-century Tel Zayit Abecedary and its inland contemporaries (the Gezer Calendar, etc.) becomes clear, especially in relation to contemporary Linear Phoenician. Although the Tel Zayit script displays substantial conformity with coastal Phoenician, it also exhibits numerous indications of independent continuity with the antecedent scripts of the Old Canaanite epigraphs of its own region, as enumerated in the list above. Finally, and paleographically most significant, the Tel Zayit script inaugurates general and specific graphic innovations that will become standard features of its regional descendant in the 9th century and later – namely, the Hebrew script. For these reasons, I have preferred to eschew the term *Phoenician* as descriptive of the Tel Zayit script in favor of the more neutral and geographically precise *south Canaanite*. From a historical perspective, the designation *Proto-Hebrew* is entirely accurate and proper in view of the fact that the sole heir to the Tel Zayit script will be the Hebrew national script, with its own daughter scripts, Moabite, Edomite, and Philistine.[11]

two Byblos clay objects of the 11th century (Cross and McCarter 1973), which might, therefore, be said to shed light only on the development of coastal Phoenician and not the contemporary inland script.

8. Lachish bowl no. 1: Diringer 1958: 129 and pls. 43–44; Cross 1954 [= Cross 2003: 309–12]. The Lachish ewer: Gaster 1940: 47–54 and frontispiece; Cross 1954 [= Cross 2003: 309–12]. The Lachish ostracon: Ussishkin 1983: 155–57 and fig. 25, pl. 40:2; Cross 1984 [= Cross 2003: 293–96].

9. Raddana jar handle: Aharoni 1971; Cross and Freedman 1971. Qubūr Walaydah inscription: Cohen 1978. Beth-shemesh ostracon: Grant 1930; 1931: pl. 10; Cross 1967: 17*–19* and fig. 3 [= Cross 2003: 324–35]. Tell eṣ-Ṣārem (Reḥov) sherd: Kallner 1945: pl. 2:1; Sukenik 1945.

10. ʿIzbet Ṣarṭah ostracon: Kochavi 1977; Demsky 1977; Naveh 1978; Cross 1980: 8–15 and figs. 9–10 [= Cross 2003: 220–27 and fig. 32.6]. Revadim (ʾAbbaʾ) seal: Giveon 1961; Cross 1962 [= Cross 2003: 299–302]. Manaḥat sherd: Stager 1969.

11. Or perhaps "Neo-Philistine," with F. M. Cross and L. E. Stager (Cross 1996b). See also Naveh 1985.

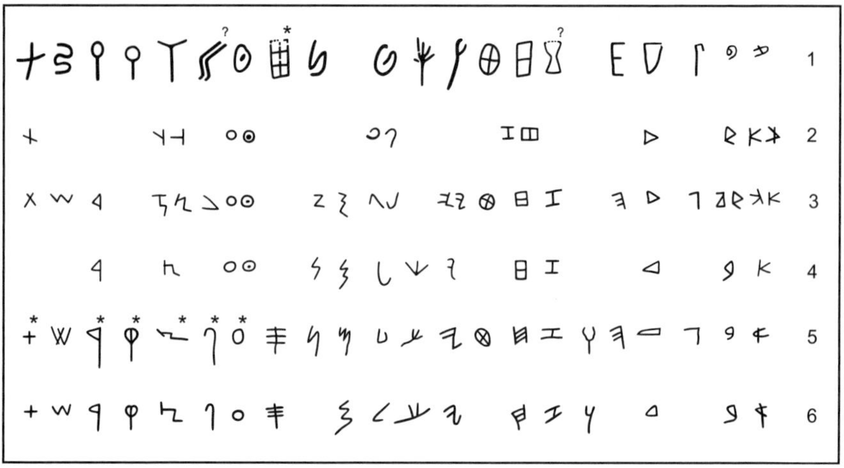

Fig. 2. Scripts of the Canaanite hinterlands (late 12th to late 10th centuries B.C.E.*).*

1. The ʿIzbet Ṣarṭah ostracon, second half of the 12th century B.C.E.
2. Bronze arrowheads, early 11th century B.C.E.
3. Bronze arrowheads, mid-11th century B.C.E.
4. Bronze arrowheads, late 11th century B.C.E.
5. The Tel Zayit Abecedary, mid-10th century B.C.E.
6. The Gezer Calendar, second half of the 10th century B.C.E.

Turning first to the matter of continuity with the earlier scripts, we note that a number of the signs in the Tel Zayit Abecedary display characteristics reminiscent of the Old Canaanite scripts of the hinterlands but lacking in contemporary coastal Phoenician. For example, the *ʾalep* of the Tel Zayit Abecedary and the Gezer Calendar does not participate in the idiosyncratic development seen uniformly in 10th-century coastal Phoenician (and also in the 11th-century arrowhead script), in which the crossbar of *ʾalep* touches the rotated V at its tip rather than intersecting it in the middle. In the older form, found, for example, in the Beth-shemesh and ʿIzbet Ṣarṭah ostraca and the Revadim (ʾAbbaʾ) seal, the crossbar intersects the V in the middle, producing an A-form (however rotated). In this respect, then, the 10th-century form of Tel Zayit and Gezer is independent of the Phoenician tradition and descended directly from the earlier form, though now with its traditional stance and the extension of the crossbar as a stem.

The broadly rounded head of the *bet* of the Tel Zayit Abecedary preserves the old form seen, for example, in the ʿIzbet Ṣarṭah ostracon, in contrast to the tightly rounded or sharp-nosed triangular heads of the *bet* of the arrowheads and the Byblian sequence. Despite a predominance of the sharp-nosed form in the script of the Meshaʿ Stele (ca. 840 B.C.E.), subsequent Hebrew shows a general preference for the rounded form, as seen for example in the stone bowl inscription from Kuntillet ʿAjrud (ca. 800 B.C.E.), though the two forms will alternate throughout the history of the script.

The headstroke of Tel Zayit *gimel* is drawn at something close to a right angle from the stem, a striking survival that recalls the form of *gimel* found in the ʿIzbet Ṣarṭah ostracon and generally in the arrowhead script but is distinct from the acute-angled headstroke of the *gimel* of the ʾAḥiram inscription and the rest of the 10th-century Byblian series. In the subsequent Hebrew script a preference for the right-angle form of *gimel* will persist, though the *gimel* of the Meshaʿ inscription has an acute angle and occasional acute-angled forms will alternate with the predominant right-angled type through the history of the script.

The narrow, compressed *dalet* of the Tel Zayit Abecedary is peculiar and probably not paleographically diagnostic, though it is paralleled in the arrowhead script and elsewhere in the archaic corpus (the Manaḥat sherd). The isosceles-triangle form of Gezer, which is similar to the coastal Phoenician form of the Byblian sequence, is the basis for subsequent development in Hebrew.

In contrast to the typologically much more developed *waw* of the Gezer Calendar, the cup-headed form of Tel Zayit *waw* conforms to and even surpasses in its archaic character the similar form of the early part of the 10th-century Byblian sequence (ʾAḥiram). Unfortunately, clear examples of *waw* are hard to find in our corpus of Old Canaanite epigraphs from the 13th to 11th centuries, so that the intermediate stages linking the 10th-century "cup"-headed *waw* to the early "mace"-headed form seen in the 13th-century Lachish ostracon and elsewhere cannot be confidently reconstructed. In any case, this "cup"-headed form of *waw* will be rapidly lost in the subsequent development of both the Phoenician and Hebrew scripts.

The script of the Gezer Calendar contains multiple examples of two types of *ḥet*, one of them a strikingly archaic survival form (Cross 1980: 18 n. 6 [= 2003: 222 n. 40]; 1986: 122 [= 2003: 257]). This latter type is the old "box"-shaped *ḥet* found, for example, in the script of the ʿIzbet Ṣarṭah ostracon, the Manaḥat sherd, and commonly in the older stages of the developing arrowhead script. In the final phase of the arrowhead script and in 10th-century coastal Phoenician, it was replaced by the "ladder"-shaped *ḥet*, which is the second type found in the Gezer Calendar and also in the Tel Zayit Abecedary.

In contrast to the *yod* of 10th-century coastal Phoenician, with its gently rounded headstroke, the *yod* of the Gezer Calendar and especially the *yod*

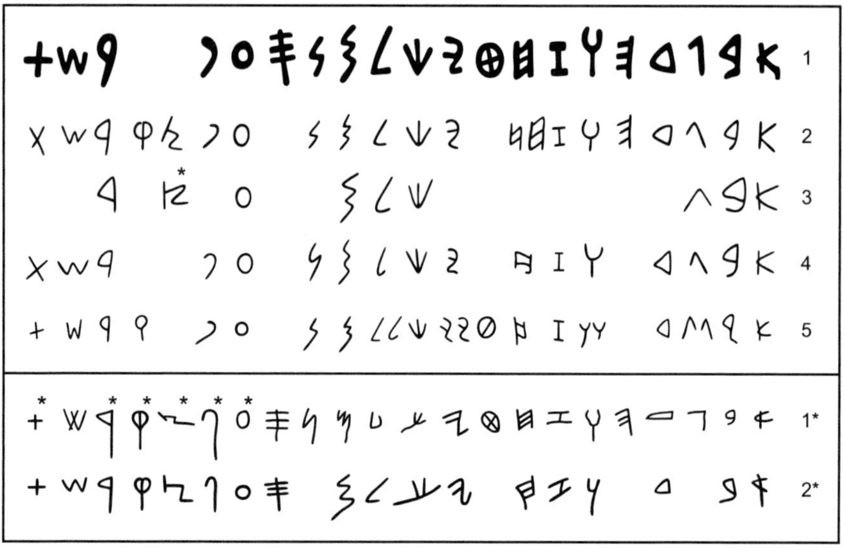

Fig. 3. The Old Byblian Script (1–5) Compared to the Tel Zayit Abecedary (1) and the Gezer Calendar (2*).*

1. The ʾAḥiram sarcophagus and tomb-shaft graffito, early 10th century B.C.E.
2. The Yeḥimilk inscription, ca. 960 B.C.E.
3. The ʾAbibaʿl inscription, ca. 940 B.C.E.
4. The ʾElibaʿl inscription, ca. 920 B.C.E.
5. The Shipiṭbaʿl inscription, ca. 900 B.C.E.

1*. The Tel Zayit Abecedary, mid-10th century B.C.E.
2*. The Gezer Calendar, second half of the 10th century B.C.E.

of the Tel Zayit Abecedary are tight and angular, continuing the prevailing pattern of the *yod* of the 11th-century arrowheads.

The *lamed* of the Tel Zayit Abecedary is remarkably archaic in appearance. It consists of a very short descending stroke that bends into a broadly curled hook, perpetuating a form last seen in the 11th-century arrowhead scripts – but commonly only in the earliest part of that series (ʾEl-Ḫaḍr) – and approaching the tightly curled form of 13th- and 12th-century scripts such as the forms of the Lachish ewer, the Raddana jar handle, the Qubūr Walaydah bowl, and the Beth-shemesh and ʿIzbet Ṣarṭah ostraca. By contrast, the *lamed* of the Gezer Calendar is unremarkable, conforming to the "checkmark" *lamed* of contemporary coastal Phoenician, in which a long, straight, descending stroke curves or angles to the right at the bottom forming a small hook. This "checkmark" form, as found in the Gezer Calendar, will become the basis for the subsequent development of Hebrew *lamed*.

The tightly coiled head of the Tel Zayit *nun* is another striking archaism, reminiscent of the head of the *nun* of the 11th-century arrowheads and the 12th-century ʿIzbet Ṣarṭah ostracon. It has no parallel in the *nun* of contemporary coastal Phoenician as represented by the Byblian series. The elongated stem of the Tel Zayit *nun*, on the other hand, is an advanced feature, as noted below. *Nun* is not found in the text of the Gezer Calendar.

The *šin* of the Gezer Calendar and especially the Tel Zayit Abecedary is large in comparison to that of contemporary coastal Phoenician, a characteristic that associates it with the rather large *šin* typical of the 11th-century arrowheads and perhaps even the large "sidelong" *šin* of the ʿIzbet Ṣarṭah ostracon. The Tel Zayit and Gezer (and contemporary Tel ʿAmal) *šin*s are all rather crudely executed. Though this crudeness is reminiscent of the *šin*s found on many of the 11th-century arrowheads and stands in clear contrast to the usually precise *šin*s of the 10th-century Byblian series, it is difficult to be sure that it is a paleographically significant survival, because the execution of the arrowhead scripts is often crude in general (see, for example, Hackett 2004: 371 §3.2.2).

If the archaisms just listed illustrate the continuity of the 10th-century inland script represented by the Tel Zayit Abecedary with its regional forbears and demonstrate a degree of independence from the coastal Phoenician tradition, the inland script's innovations in relation both to the older regional scripts and the coastal Phoenician tradition point to its role as the root of subsequent south Canaanite script development and, in particular, the progenitor of the Hebrew script of the 9th century B.C.E. To speak of the script of the Tel Zayit Abecedary and the Gezer Calendar as the progenitor of the Hebrew script is not to suggest that these two 10th-century inscriptions should be classified as Hebrew, a classification that in my view would be a mistake (see the cautious remarks of Cross 1980: 14 [= Cross 2003: 226]). The diagnostic features of the Hebrew script appear unambiguously only in the 9th or even 8th century (Naveh 1982: 65–66).

Nevertheless, it seems possible to identify certain general and specific features of the scripts of the 10th-century Tel Zayit and Gezer inscriptions that anticipate aspects of the genuine Hebrew development that followed. Among the specifics, at least the following may be noted. The *zayin* of the Tel Zayit Abecedary is symmetrical (contrast the Gezer Calendar form) and very broad. Both the Tel Zayit and Gezer forms of *zayin* show a shortening of the vertical stroke in comparison with the tall form of coastal Phoenician *zayin*, as seen in the Byblian series. In all these respects, the 10th-century inland form of *zayin* anticipates the Hebrew development, in which the horizontal strokes tend to be long and the vertical quite short. Unfortunately, it is difficult to tell whether the character of the 10th-century form of *zayin* is the result of a survival of archaic characteristics, because earlier examples are not extant, and the analysis is complicated by the use of the grapheme to represent the recently merged consonants *δ and **z*.

While the "trident"-form *kap* is found consistently in the scripts of the 11th-century arrowheads and 10th-century coastal Phoenician, the Tel Zayit Abecedary and Gezer Calendar already have the form with the right stroke of the "trident" elongated into a stem. In Phoenician, this form replaces the "trident"-form type in the 9th century, but the replacement is accompanied by a counterclockwise rotation, which is lacking in the 10th-century Tel Zayit and Gezer form. It is noteworthy that the *kap* of the mature Hebrew script will also lack the counterclockwise rotation that came to characterize Phoenician *kap*.

The archaic *mem* of the Gezer Calendar corresponds to the 10th-century Phoenician form or, according to Cross (1980: 18 n. 16 [= Cross 2003: 222 n. 40]), even the 11th-century Proto-Canaanite form, consisting of five upright strokes with little head formation or elongation of the fifth stroke as a stem. By contrast, the *mem* of the Tel Zayit Abecedary anticipates to a remarkable degree the much more advanced form of the 9th-century Hebrew script. The head has rotated into the position of its subsequent development, and the stem has elongated accordingly, so that 9th-century Hebrew *mem*, as seen in the Meshaʿ Stele (ca. 840 B.C.E.), departs from the Tel Zayit antetype only in the graceful curve of the descendant stem in the Meshaʿ script, a characteristic that will persist in Hebrew *mem* throughout its history.

The *ṣade* of the script of the Gezer Calendar and probably of the Tel Zayit Abecedary has a notably short vertical base stroke, a characteristic shared with early Phoenician *ṣade*. While this stroke lengthens dramatically in its subsequent Phoenician development, it remains short in Hebrew, as seen in the script of the Meshaʿ Stele (ca. 840 B.C.E.) – a trait that persists in Hebrew into the 8th century and down to the end of the Hebrew script.

Finally, we note the tendency in the early Northwest Semitic scripts and those derived from them (such as Greek) toward elongation of the vertical body strokes and, where they exist, the stems. This issue is of general relevance to the question of the relationship of the 10th-century script of Tel Zayit and Gezer to the Hebrew script of the 9th to 8th centuries and later, because not one but several graphemes are affected. This phenomenon (stem elongation) has special paleographical significance for comparison of the developing Phoenician, Aramaic, and Hebrew traditions. Early Linear Phoenician with its lapidary successor shows most resistance to the

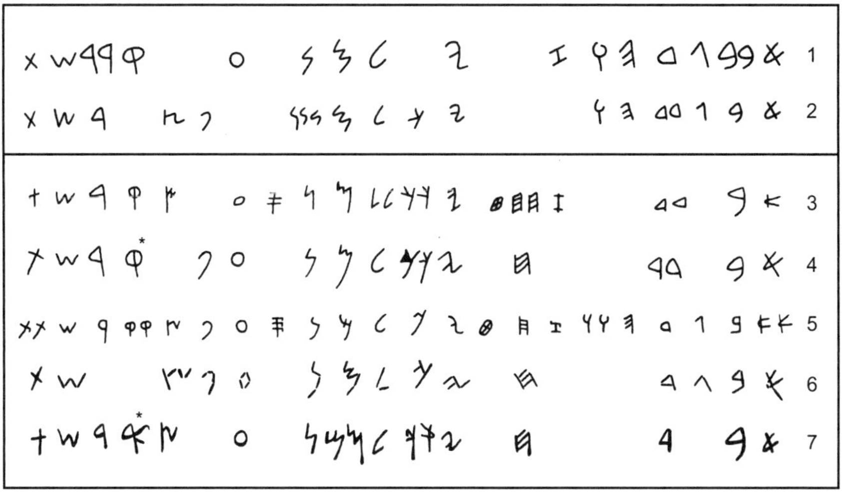

Fig. 4. Phoenician Lapidary Scripts of the 9th and 8th Centuries B.C.E.

1. The Honeyman inscription (*KAI* 30), Cyprus, first half of the 9th century B.C.E.
2. The Nora Stone (*KAI* 46), Sardinia, second half of the 9th century B.C.E.
3. The Baʿl Lebanon inscription (*KAI* 31), third quarter of the 8th century B.C.E.
4. Seville statuette (*Hispania* 14), Spain, second half of the 8th century B.C.E.
5. Karatepe inscriptions (*KAI* 26), ca. 725 B.C.E.
6. Gold pendant (*KAI* 73), Carthage, late 8th century B.C.E.
7. Malta stele (*KAI* 61A), late 8th century B.C.E.

tendency by remaining symmetrical and compact throughout the 10th and 9th centuries. In the 9th century, short stems begin to appear on certain Phoenician forms, such as *dalet*, *he* (already in the 10th), *mem*, and *ṣade*, but the elongation of these stems, as of other vertical features of the Phoenician script, does not make its appearance until the 8th to 7th centuries and later.

In striking contrast to the situation in Phoenician is the early elongation of the letter forms of the scripts of the Syrian and Canaanite heartland. In Aramaic, the primary period of elongation is the 9th century B.C.E., at least a century earlier than in Phoenician. Thus 9th-century Aramaic *ʾalep* is sometimes notably elongated (Bir-Hadad, mid-9th century B.C.E.; Kilamuwa, ca. 825 B.C.E.).

The stemless triangular form of 10th-century Phoenician *dalet* is also found in at least one Aramaic *dalet* of the beginning of the 9th century

(Gozan Pedestal, ca. 900 B.C.E.), but over the course of the 9th century the shaft descends, thus forming a well-defined stem (Bir-Hadad and ʿAmman Citadel, mid-9th century B.C.E.; Tel Dan Stele, ca. 840 B.C.E.; Kilamuwa, ca. 825 B.C.E.). Similarly, the stem of 9th-century Aramaic *he* has become noticeably elongated (Bir-Hadad, ca. 850 B.C.E.; Tel Dan Stele, ca. 840 B.C.E.). The single surviving Aramaic inscription from the beginning of the 9th century (Gozan Pedestal, ca. 900 B.C.E.) displays an upright, reverse-K-form *kap*, reminiscent of the *kap* of the late-9th-century B.C.E. Phoenician Nora stone. In the course of its own 9th-century development, however, the stem of Aramaic *kap* becomes increasingly elongated (ʿAmman Citadel, mid-9th century B.C.E.; Kilamuwa, ca. 825 B.C.E.).

The elongation of the base stroke of *ṣade* observed in Phoenician inscriptions of the 8th and 7th centuries B.C.E. is already present in Aramaic in the 9th century B.C.E. (Bir-Hadad, ca. 850 B.C.E.; Kilamuwa, ca. 825 B.C.E.). Ninth-century Aramaic *taw* developed from an X-shaped form similar to the *taw* of 10th-century Phoenician as the result of a slight counterclockwise rotation accompanied by substantial elongation of the left lower stroke (Bir-Hadad, ca. 850 B.C.E.; ʿAmman Citadel, mid-9th century B.C.E.; Tel Dan Stele, ca. 840 B.C.E.; Kilamuwa, ca. 825 B.C.E.), a development that occurred much later in Phoenician.

The Hebrew script, like the Aramaic, shows a tendency toward stem elongation in the 9th century B.C.E., as shown by the following examples. In the script of the Meshaʿ Stele (ca. 840 B.C.E.) the stem of *ʾalep* is elongated. The 9th-century Hebrew forms of *he* also show stem elongation, with the exception of the conservative *he* of the Kuntillet ʿAjrud stone bowl (ca. 800 B.C.E.), which in other graphemes (*bet, waw, kap, nun, reš*) exhibits a pattern of stem elongation well advanced beyond contemporary Phoenician (Cross 1980: 18 n. 16 [= Cross 2003: 222 n. 40). Ninth-century Hebrew *kap* shares with contemporary Aramaic *kap* the tendency toward elongation of the stem, which in the Hebrew tradition tends to curve or even curl upward (Meshaʿ Stele, ca. 840 B.C.E.; Kuntillet ʿAjrud pithoi, early 8th-century B.C.E.).

Thus the elongation of letter forms in the Tel Zayit Abecedary and the Gezer Calendar is one of the principal reasons I have emphasized that the script of these two inscriptions "already exhibits characteristics that anticipate the distinctive features of the Hebrew national script" (Tappy et al. 2006: 26–28). The alphabetic signs that exhibit this elongation in the Tel Zayit Abecedary include especially *ʾalep*, *he*, *waw*, *kap*, *mem*, *nun*, and (very tentatively) *reš*.[12]

12. A similar listing of Gezer Calendar forms showing elongation would include *ʾalep*, *kap*, *mem*, *samek*, *pe*, *qop* and *reš* (Cross 1980: 14 [= Cross 2003: 226]; 1993: 540 n. 5 [= Cross 2003: 208 n. 5]).

Bibliography

Aharoni, Y.
1971 Khirbet Raddana and Its Inscription. *IEJ* 21: 130–35.
AHI = Davies 1991
Bordreuil, P.
1992 Flèches phéniciennes inscrites: 1981–1991. *RB* 99: 205–13 and pls. 2–3.
Bunimovitz, S., and Lederman, Z.
1997a Six Seasons of Excavations at Tel Beth-Shemesh: A City on the Border of Judah. *Qadmoniot* 30: 22–37. [Hebrew]
1997b Beth-Shemesh: Culture Conflict on Judah's Frontier. *BAR* 23/1: 42–49, 75–77.
Cohen, R.
1978 Qubur el-Walaida. *IEJ* 28: 194–95.
Cross, F. M.
1954 The Evolution of the Proto-Canaanite Alphabet. *BASOR* 134: 15–24. [Repr. Cross 2003: 309–12]
1962 An Archaic Inscribed Seal from the Valley of Aijalon [Soreq]. *BASOR* 168: 12–18. [Repr. Cross 2003: 299–302]
1967 The Origin and Early Evolution of the Alphabet. *ErIsr* 8 (Sukenik Volume): 8*–24*. [Repr. Cross 2003: 317–29]
1979 Early Alphabetic Scripts. Pp. 95–123 in *Symposia Celebrating the Seventy-Fifth Anniversary of the Founding of the American Schools of Oriental Research (1900–1975): Archaeology and Early Israelite History*, ed. F. M. Cross. Cambridge, MA: American Schools of Oriental Research. [Repr. Cross 2003: 330–43]
1980 Newly Found Inscriptions in Old Canaanite and Early Phoenician Scripts. *BASOR* 238: 1–20. [Repr. Cross 2003: 213–30]
1984 An Old Caananite Inscription Newly Found at Lachish. *TA* 11: 71–76.
1986 Phoenicians in the West: The Early Epigraphic Evidence. Pp. 116–30 in *Studies in Sardinian Archaeology II*, ed. M. S. Balmuth. Ann Arbor: University of Michigan Press. [Repr. Cross 2003: 254–59]
1993 Newly Discovered Inscribed Arrowheads of the 11th Century B.C.E. Pp. 533–42 in *Biblical Archaeology Today, 1990*, ed. A. Biran and J. Aviram. Proceedings of the Second International Congress on Biblical Archaeology. Jerusalem: Israel Exploration Society. [Repr. Cross 2003: 207–12]
1996a The Arrow of Suwar, Retainer of ʿAbday. *ErIsr* 25 (Aviram Volume): 9*–17*. [Repr. Cross 2003: 195–202]
1996b A Philistine Ostracon from Ashkelon. *BAR* 22: 64–65.
2003 *Leaves from an Epigrapher's Notebook: Collected Papers in Hebrew and West Semitic Palaeography and Epigraphy.* HSS 51. Winona Lake, IN: Eisenbrauns.
Cross, F. M., and Freedman, D. N.
1971 An Inscribed Jar Handle from Raddana. *BASOR* 201: 19–22.
Cross, F. M., and McCarter, P. K.
1973 Two Archaic Inscriptions on Clay Objects from Byblus. *Rivista di studi fenici* 1: 3–8.

Cross, F. M., and Milik, J. T.

1954 Inscribed Javelin-Heads from the Period of the Judges. *BASOR* 134: 5–15. [Repr. Cross 2003: 303–8]

Davies, G. I.

1991 *Ancient Hebrew Inscriptions: Corpus and Concordance.* Cambridge: Cambridge University Press.

Demsky, A.

1977 A Proto-Canaanite Abecedary Dating from the Period of the Judges and Its Implications for the History of the Alphabet. *TA* 4: 14–27.

Deutsch, R., and Heltzer, M.

1997 *Windows to the Past.* Tel Aviv–Jaffa: Archaeological Center.

1999 *West Semitic Epigraphic News of the 1st Millennium* BCE. Tel Aviv–Jaffa: Archaeological Center.

Diringer, D.

1958 Inscriptions. Pp. 127–31 in *Lachish IV (Tell ed-Duweir): The Bronze Age,* ed. O. Tufnell. London: Oxford University Press.

Dobbs-Alsopp, F. W.; Roberts, J. J. M.; Seow, C. L.; and Whitaker, R. E.

2005 *Hebrew Inscriptions: Texts from the Biblical Period of the Monarchy with Concordance.* New Haven, CT: Yale University Press.

Donner, H., and Röllig, W.

1962–64 *Kanaanäische und aramäische Inschriften.* 3 vols. Wiesbaden: Harrassowitz.

Gaster, T. H.

1940 The Archaic Inscriptions. Pp. 49–57 in *Lachish II (Tell ed-Duweir): The Fosse Temple,* ed. O. Tufnell. London: Oxford University Press.

Gibson, J. C. L.

1971–82 *Textbook of Syrian Semitic Inscriptions.* 3 vols. Oxford: Clarendon.

Giveon, R.

1961 Two New Hebrew Seals and Their Iconographic Background. *PEQ* 93: 38–39.

Grant, E.

1930 Découverte épigraphique à Beth Šemeš. *RB* 39: 228–29.

1931 *Ain Shems Excavation I.* Haverford College Biblical and Kindred Studies 3. Haverford: Haverford College Press.

Hackett, J. A.

2004 Phoenician and Punic. Pp. 365–85 in *The Cambridge Encyclopedia of the World's Ancient Languages,* ed. R. D. Woodard. Cambridge: Cambridge University Press.

HAE = Renz and Röllig 1992

HI = Dobbs-Alsopp et al. 2005

KAI = Donner and Röllig 1962–64

Kallner, R. B.

1945 Two Inscribed Sherds. *Qedem* 2: 11–14. [Hebrew]

Kelm, G. L., and Mazar, A.

1991 Tel Batash (Timnah) Excavations: Third Preliminary Report (1984–1989). Pp. 47–67 in *Preliminary Reports of ASOR-Sponsored Excavations,*

1982–89. BASORSup 27. Baltimore: Johns Hopkins University Press for the American Schools of Oriental Research.
1995 *Timnah: A Biblical City in the Sorek Valley.* Winona Lake, IN: Eisenbrauns.

Kochavi, M.
1977 An Ostracon of the Period of the Judges from ʿIzbet Ṣarṭah. *TA* 4: 1–13.

Levy, S., and Edelstein, G.
1972 Cinq saisons de fouilles à Tel ʿAmal (Nir David). *RB* 79: 325–67.

Mazar, A.
2003 Three 10th–9th Century Inscriptions from *Tēl Reḥôv*. Pp. 171–84 in *Saxa loquentur: Studien zur Archäologie Palästinas/Israels. Festschrift für Volkmar Fritz zum 65. Geburtstag,* ed. C. G. den Hertog, U. Hübner, and S. Münger. AOAT 302. Münster: Ugarit-Verlag.

McCarter, P. K.
1996 *Ancient Inscriptions: Voices from the Biblical World.* Washington, DC: Biblical Archaeology Society.
1999 Two Bronze Arrowheads with Archaic Alphabetic Inscriptions. *ErIsr* 26 (Cross Volume): 123*–28*.

Naveh, J.
1978 Some Considerations on the Ostracon from ʿIzbet Ṣarṭah. *IEJ* 28: 31–35.
1982 *Early History of the Alphabet: An Introduction to West Semitic Epigraphy and Palaeography.* Jerusalem: Magnes / Leiden: Brill.
1985 Writing and Scripts in Seventh-Century BCE Philistia: The New Evidence from Tell Jemmeh. *IEJ* 35: 8–21.

Pritchard, J. B.
1975 *Sarepta: A Preliminary Report on the Iron Age.* Philadelphia: University Museum Press.

Renz, J., and Röllig, W.
1992 *Handbuch der althebräischen Epigraphik.* 3 vols. Darmstadt: Wissenschaftliche.

Stager, L. E.
1969 An Inscribed Potsherd from the Eleventh Century. *BASOR* 194: 45–52.

Sukenik, E. L.
1945 Note on the Sherd from Tell eṣ-Ṣārem. *Qedem* 2: 15. [Hebrew]

Tappy, R. E.; McCarter, P. K.; Lundberg, M.; and Zuckerman, B.
2006 An Abecedary of the Mid-Tenth Century from the Judaean Shephelah. *BASOR* 344: 5–46.

TSSI = Gibson 1971–82

Ussishkin, D.
1983 Excavations at Lachish 1978–1983: Second Preliminary Report. *TA* 10: 97–185.

The Phoenician Script of the Tel Zayit Abecedary and Putative Evidence for Israelite Literacy

CHRISTOPHER A. ROLLSTON
Emmanuel School of Religion, a Graduate Seminary

Literacy: Ancient and Modern

The definition of literacy for antiquity (and modernity) is the subject of substantial debate. Some suggest that in "oral cultures" the capacity to use language (that is, the spoken word) in a functional or sophisticated manner constitutes literacy. However, some wish to argue that literacy is a term that is to be understood as referring to the ability to read and write texts. Occasionally, there are those who propose that functional literacy be defined as just the capacity to write one's name. The United Nations Educational Scientific and Cultural Organization (UNESCO) has produced the following minimalist definition for the contemporary period: "Literacy is the ability to read and write with understanding a simple statement related to one's daily life. It involves a continuum of reading and writing skills, and often includes also basic arithmetic skills (numeracy)."[1] The bibliography for the subject of literacy in antiquity (and modernity) is vast and varied.[2]

For the southern Levant during antiquity, (1) I propose the following as a working description of *literacy*: substantial facility in a writing system, that is, the ability to write and read, using and understanding a standard script, a standard orthography, a standard numeric system, conventional formatting and terminology, and with minimal errors (of composition or comprehension). Moreover, I maintain that the capacity to scrawl one's name on a contract, but without the ability to write or read anything else

1. This definition is provided in a UNESCO position paper entitled "The Plurality of Literacy and Its Implications for Policies and Programmes."

2. For some discussion and bibliography, see Treiman and Kessler 2005; Seymour 2005; B. Byrne 2005; Frost 2005. For bibliography and discussion on the world of ancient Israel, see especially Niditch 1996; Schniedewind 2004; Carr 2005; Rollston forthcoming a.

is not literacy – not even some sort of "functional literacy." Rather, individuals with this low level of capability should be classed as illiterate. (2) However, I also argue that there were some in ancient Israel who should be classed as semiliterates. That is, there were ostensibly those who were capable of reading the most remedial texts with at least a modest level of comprehension and often the ability to pen some of the most common and simple words. (3) Naturally, I also posit that there was much variation within each of these categories, but precise penetration into the nature of this variation is not something that the data (ancient or modern) can accomplish.

Since the discovery and publication of the Tel Zayit Abecedary (Tappy et al. 2006), there has been discussion about its import for the subject of literacy in the 10th century and early 9th century B.C.E. Of particular interest is the argument that the Tel Zayit Abecedary can serve as evidence supporting the notion of widespread literacy in ancient Israel. Thus, within an article that uses the Tel Zayit Abecedary as an *Ausgangspunkt*, Hess states the following: "The announcement of the discovery of a tenth century B.C.E. abecedary . . . provides further opportunity for reflecting on the development of literacy in ancient Israel." Hess believes that the abecedary "served the purposes of learning how to read and write in Hebrew." Then – and this is a critical point – he affirms that the Tel Zayit Abecedary augments his arguments and "serves to emphasize the presence of numerous writers and readers of Hebrew, and perhaps other neighboring scripts." He posits that "the effect is to increase the evidence for the presence of a literacy that could be found in rural areas as well as in state capitals and administrative centers" (Hess 2006: 342–43).

Within this article, he also refers to monumental display inscriptions and affirms, "the presence of such inscriptions assumes that a significant number of people could read them." Most significantly, he also states that he believes there is "continually increasing evidence for a wide variety of people from all walks of life who could read and write." In addition, he affirms that he believes "the whole picture is consistent with a variety of [literate] classes and groups, not merely a few elites." For Hess, the Tel Zayit Abecedary functions as a "dramatic attestation" to the "increasing evidence for the presence of writing during the Israelite monarchy" and also attests to the "early and ongoing presence of readers and writers at many levels of Israelite society."

Making his position crystal clear, he states that the epigraphic evidence "argues against the view that only priests, government officials, and professional scribes could read or write" (Hess 2006: 345 n. 10). Obviously, Hess is here arguing that both elites and non-elites were literate in ancient Israel. Hess's prior work contains similar statements: "it is not possible to limit those who wrote and read to specific classes or places," and "there is no evidence from the epigraphy to assume that members of any class could not learn how to read and write" (Hess 2002: 95).[3] Moreover, Hess (2002; 2006) is very critical of Young's tandem articles that argue that within the Hebrew Bible it is elites who are portrayed as reading and writing (Young 1998a; 1998b; cf. 2005). Nevertheless, I argue that Hess's conclusions about widespread non-elite literacy are too broad and sweeping to be considered accurate constructs of the epigraphic evidence, including the Tel Zayit Abecedary.

To be sure, it is readily apparent that the Tel Zayit Abecedary should be considered an important component of discussions about writing and literacy in the southern Levant for some time to come. Moreover, this abecedary serves as further evidence demonstrating that there was indeed *some* literacy in this region during this chronological horizon. However, the Tel Zayit Abecedary certainly cannot be used as an epigraphic basis for assuming the "early and ongoing presence of readers and writers at many levels of Israelite society." That is, on the basis of a single abecedary, it is not methodologically tenable to attempt to draw conclusions about the rough percentage of people who were literate (that is, *pace* Hess and his "numerous writers and readers"), nor can conclusions be drawn about the non-elite social status of writers and readers at Zayit (that is, *pace* Hess and his "not merely a few elites" and his "wide variety of people from all walks of life"). Hess might retort that it is the cumulative evidence that suggests that nonelites were literate as well. However, I believe, based on the epigraphic evidence, that this conclusion is also much too sanguine (Rollston 2006).

The Obvious Dearth of Linguistic Data in Abecedaries

Much is known about the lexemes and morphemes in Iron Age Northwest Semitic.[4] However, because the inscription from Tel Zayit is an abecedary, it has no lexemes or morphemes. There is a substantial body of literature focusing on affixes (prefixes, suffixes, infixes) and syntagms in

---

3. There are some severe tensions (that is, inconsistencies) within Hess's cited article. Thus, immediately after writing the statement cited here, he also writes, "the question of how widespread literacy was cannot be answered on the basis of the present evidence" (Hess 2002: 95). With justification, one could refer to such statements as "Hess against himself."

4. See, for example, Hoftijzer and Jongeling 1995 (Iron Age Epigraphic Northwest Semitic); Koehler and Baumgartner 1994–2000 (Biblical Hebrew); compare with del Olmo Lete and Sanmartín 2004 (Ugaritic) for Late Bronze Age cognate data.

	*PS	Phoenician	Hebrew	Aramaic
1.	ʾ	ʾ	ʾ	ʾ
2.	b	b	b	b
3.	g	g	g	g
4.	d	d	d	d
5.	h	h	h	h
6.	w	w (y)	w (y)	w (y)
7.	ḏ	z	z	z/d
8.	z	z	z	z
9.	ḥ	ḥ	ḥ	ḥ
10.	ḫ	ḥ	ḥ	ḥ
11.	ṭ	ṭ	ṭ	ṭ
12.	y	y	y	y
13.	k	k	k	k
14.	l	l	l	l
15.	m	m	m	m
16.	n	n	n	n
17.	s	s	s	s
18.	ʿ	ʿ	ʿ	ʿ
19.	ġ	ʿ	ʿ	ʿ
20.	p	p	p	p
21.	ṣ	ṣ	ṣ	ṣ
22.	ẓ	ṣ	ṣ	ṣ/ṭ
23.	ḍ	ṣ	ṣ	q/ʿ
24.	q	q	q	q
25.	r	r	r	r
26.	ś	š	ś	š
27.	š	š	š	š
28.	ṯ	š	š	š/t
29.	t	t	t	t

Fig. 1. Semitic consonants.

Iron Age Northwest Semitic.[5] However, because the Tel Zayit inscription is an abecedary, it contains no affixes and no syntagms. Much is also known about the orthography of Iron Age Northwest Semitic inscriptions

5. Friedrich and Röllig 1999 (Phoenician); Segert 1976 (Phoenician); Degen 1969 (Aramaic); Segert 1975 (Aramaic); Joüon 1993 (Biblical Hebrew); Waltke and O'Connor 1990 (Biblical Hebrew); Gogel 1998 (Epigraphic Hebrew); compare with Segert 1984 (Ugaritic); Tropper 2000 (Ugaritic) for Late Bronze Age cognate data.

(Cross and Freedman 1952; 1975; Zevit 1980; Garr 1985; Rollston 2006). However, because the Tel Zayit inscription is an abecedary, it provides no orthographic data. Of course, because the Tel Zayit inscription is an abecedary, nothing can be deduced about aspects of morphology, such as the means of pluralizing (for example, nouns, adjectives, verbs), or about the means of determining forms (for example, prepositive article or postpositive article). In sum, although there is much paleographic data in an abecedary, there is a distinct dearth of linguistic data.

Someone might argue, however, that the Tel Zayit Abecedary does provide some phonological data. After all, there are a total of 22 letters in this abecedary, and this fact demonstrates that various consonantal mergers had occurred. Obviously, the Tel Zayit Abecedary does employ the 22-letter alphabet, which is the norm in linear alphabetic Northwest Semitic of the Iron Age (Garr 1985; Z. S. Harris 1939). However, because these letters are employed in an abecedary rather than a "verbal" text (that is, a text with words), nothing can be deduced about phonological isoglosses.

That is, (1) for example, within Canaanite, Proto-Semitic *ḍ* > *ṣ*; thus *ṣʾn* is the Canaanite form of a word for 'sheep' (compare with Phoenician *ṣʾn*; Hebrew *ṣʾn*; Moabite *ṣʾn*; Ammonite *ṣʾn* [Heshbon A1: 2]; and note also Ugaritic *ṣin*).[6] The *ṣade* of this word is not etymological, however. Rather, the Proto-Semitic root is *ḍʾn* (compare with Old South Arabic and Classical Arabic *ḍʾn*). Within Old Aramaic, Proto-Semitic *ḍ* > *q* (for example, Old Aramaic *ʾrq* 'earth' for an original Proto-Semitic *ʾrḍ*). Within later Aramaic, *ḍ* > *ʿ* (for example, Palmyrene, Nabatean, and Jewish Aramaic *ʾrʿ*). Imperial Aramaic preserves both *ʾrq* and *ʾrʿ*.[7] Note the word *ʿnʾ* ('sheep') in Jewish Aramaic, with *ʿayin* a reflex of the original *ḍ* but with the metathesis of the *nun* and *ʾalep*. Based on the Tel Zayit Abecedary, however, nothing can be deduced regarding this phonological isogloss (that is, there is nothing in the abecedary itself that would allow modern linguists to make determinations regarding the dialect of the writer of the Tel Zayit Abecedary).

(2) The phonological evidence for etymological *ṯ* can also be considered useful for the classification of a Northwest Semitic text. Within Iron Age Canaanite, Proto-Semitic *ṯ* > *š*; thus *šwb* is the Canaanite form of a

6. The fact that the Canaanite gloss in El Amarna 263.12 is written *ṣunu*, that is, without *ʾalep*, is a reflection of the general limitations of using Mesopotamian cuneiform to write certain Northwest Semitic graphemes and phonemes (for the Amarna Letters, see Moran 1992; Rainey 1996).

7. Note that the MT of Jer 10:11 contains Aramaic and preserves both spellings, a deft piece of literary artistry also reflective of the fact that this period was one of phonological transition for *ḍ*.

word for 'return' (compare with Hebrew *šwb*; Moabite *šwb*). The *šin* of this word is not etymological, however. Rather, the Proto-Semitic root is *ṯwb* (compare with Ugaritic *ṯwb*, Old South Arabic *ṯwb*, Classical Arabic *ṯwb*). Within Old Aramaic, Proto-Semitic *ṯ* > *š* (for example, Old Aramaic *šwb*; Old Aramaic *yšb*), but within later Aramaic *ṯ* > *t* (Biblical Aramaic *twb*, *ytb*).[8] Within Ammonite, the seal of Šub'il (J 1195 = Aufrecht 1989: #41) contains a theophoric *'il* and (arguably) the verbal root *šwb*.[9] Based on the Tel Zayit Abecedary, however, nothing can be deduced regarding this phonological isogloss.

(3) The phonological evidence for etymological *ḏ* is also useful to Northwest Semitic linguists attempting to discern isoglosses. Within Iron Age Canaanite, Proto-Semitic *ḏ* > *z*; thus *ʿzr* is the Canaanite form of a word for 'help' (for example, Hebrew *ʿzr*, Phoenician *ʿzr*). The *zayin* of this word is not etymological. Rather, the Proto-Semitic root is *ʿḏr* (compare with Ugaritic *ʿḏr*, Old South Arabic *ʿḏr* and Classical Arabic *ʿḏr*). Within Old Aramaic, Proto-Semitic *ḏ* > *z* (for example, Old Aramaic *zqn* 'old' from an original Proto-Semitic *ḏqn*), but within later Aramaic *ḏ* > *d* (for example, *dhb* 'gold' from an original Proto-Semitic *ḏhb*, and Palmyrene *ʿdr* from an original Proto-Semitic *ʿḏr*). The ʿAmman Statue Inscription (J 1656 = Aufrecht 1989: #43) contains the personal name *yrḥʿzr*, thus arguably patterning with Canaanite and also with Old Aramaic but not with later Aramaic.

In sum, when working with texts that contain Northwest Semitic lexemes and morphemes, we can make determinations about phonological isoglosses; however, *in an abecedary there are no lexemes and morphemes* (etc.); therefore, there is no secure basis for discussion of phonological isoglosses. To be sure, we can state that the Tel Zayit Abecedary is alphabetic Iron Age Northwest Semitic with 22 consonants, but to be able to make this statement is of truly modest usefulness. That is, the data that are the desiderata for making determinations about the linguistic classification of

8. Notice that the Old Aramaic Tell Fakhariyeh Statue Inscription uses *samek* to represent *ṯ* (Abou-Assaf, Bordreuil, and Millard 1982; Kaufman 1982: 146–47). Kaufman astutely notes that, in a technical sense, this issue is orthographic rather than phonological. That is, the interdental *ṯ* was still pronounced and the scribe of Fakhariyeh chose the grapheme *samek* to represent the phoneme *ṯ*. However, within Old Aramaic, the normal custom was for the scribes to use the grapheme *š* to represent *ṯ*. See also Garr 1985: 28–29.

9. I use the term "arguably" because it would be possible to suggest that the root is actually *yšb*, but because the *šin* of this root comes from an original *ṯ* my point is not affected, regardless of whether one views the Ammonite personal name as employing the root *yšb* or the root *ṯwb*. For discussion of imperative forms in personal names, see O'Connor 1990: 155–56.

an Iron Age Northwest Semitic language (or dialect) are simply not present in an abecedary. We need lexemes and morphemes for this task, and we simply do not have them.[10] In short, for an inscription to be used as a putative component of an argument for widespread non-elite literacy, it would need to provide a great deal of data (linguistic, historical, social), but the Tel Zayit inscription is an abecedary and thus lacks these data. For this reason, I am very disinclined to see it used as a component of discussions about the extent or nature of literacy.

Assumptions about Alphabetic Writing and the Pace of Learning

The writing systems developed and employed in ancient Mesopotamia and Egypt were complex, nonalphabetic systems with large inventories of signs. Scholars have argued that, for even the most assiduous students, developing substantial facility in these writing systems required years of arduous training.[11] Conversely, it has normally been argued that the mastery of linear alphabetic Northwest Semitic was facile, requiring just days or weeks of training. Regarding the Old Hebrew alphabet, for example, Albright stated that, "since the forms of the letters are very simple, the 22-letter alphabet could be learned in a day or two by a bright student and in a week or two by the dullest." He proceeded to affirm that he did "not doubt for a moment that there were many urchins in various parts of Palestine who could read and write as early as the time of the Judges" (Albright 1960: 123).

Jamieson-Drake has opined that the Old Hebrew alphabet was "simple enough that functional knowledge of it could be passed on from one person to another in a comparatively short time" and that "schools would

10. Obviously, my working assumption is that the writer of the Tel Zayit Abecedary spoke a Canaanite language, but the point is that we cannot establish this point securely on the basis of an abecedary.

11. I concur that mastering an alphabetic writing system is not as difficult as mastering Mesopotamian cuneiform or Egyptian hieroglyphics, but to suggest that it is facile to become proficient in one's *first* alphabetic writing system is not tenable. For discussion and bibliography on "schools" in ancient Egypt, see especially Brunner 1991; Janssen and Janssen 1990; McDowell 1999; 2000. For Mesopotamia, see especially Vanstiphout 1979; Tinney 1998; 1999; Veldhuis 2003; George 2005 (see also the bibliography in Rollston 2001). Certainly the consensus of research is that learning the writing systems for hieroglyphs and cuneiform was an arduous venture for the ancients. Also of import, though, are some recent studies that have actually argued that there are numerous variables, so "attempts to describe writing systems along a simple continuum of difficulty are inadequate" (Lee, Uttal, and Chen 1995).

hardly have been necessary" (Jamieson-Drake 1991: 154, 156). Weeks states, "[that] the Phoenician alphabet [was] adopted and then adapted in Israel is neither complicated nor arcane, and it is not necessary to suppose that lengthy schooling and a course in reading literature was necessary for a good grasp of the essentials" (Weeks 1994: 151; cf. Crenshaw 1998: 107). Writers who posit high levels of literacy across the socioeconomic spectrum for the Iron Age Levant normally assume (sometimes stated, sometimes not) that the linear alphabet was so easy that high rates of literacy can be assumed.

However, I argue that assumptions about the simplicity of the linear-alphabetic Northwest Semitic writing system and the rapidity of the pace at which proficiency could have been achieved are much too sanguine (Rollston 2006: 48–49). Note that, rather than positing rapid proficiency in alphabetic writing, recent empirical studies of modern languages have delineated developmental phases ("stages") in the process of word-reading and word-spelling (Henderson 1985; Ehri 1997; 1998; Seymour 1997; Richgels 2002; Beech 2005).[12] Furthermore, it has been argued on the basis of these empirical studies that for children to become proficient in a modern writing system (that is, their first writing system) a few years are normally required, not a few days or weeks (Henderson 1985; Ehri 2002). Of course, it is readily apparent that emergent writing ("bare-bones literacy") is often attested within "initial" periods of instruction, but proficiency (for example, capacity to produce "documents" with minimal orthographic errors and with the letters reflecting accurate morphology and stance as well as standard relative size) requires substantial time.[13]

12. Ehri summarizes these stages in broad terms as follows: (1) prealphabetic, (2) partial alphabetic, (3) full alphabetic, (4) consolidated alphabetic. The first stage applies to "prereaders who operate with nonalphabetic information because they know little about the alphabetic system." The second stage applies to "novice beginners who operate with rudimentary knowledge of some letter-sound relations." The third level applies to students who "possess more complete knowledge involving grapheme-phoneme units and how these units form words." The fourth level "applies to more advanced students who have knowledge of letter patterns as well as grapheme-phoneme units" (Ehri 1997: 240, 253–56).

13. Reading and writing are cognate, but different, skills. Note that writing requires not only the ability to recognize letters but also the capacity to produce them. In addition, it requires the capacity to spell words in the conventional manner (for example, without morphological metathesis and with the correct consonants and vowels in the conventional lexical positions). In essence, although there is a strong correlative structure between spelling and reading, there is also a general asymmetry between them (cf. Bosman and van Orden 1997; Ehri 1997).

Naturally, some alphabetic writing systems are more difficult to master. For example, modern languages with a deep orthography (for example, English, Danish) arguably require more time for the achievement of proficiency than languages with a shallow(er) orthography (for example, German, Finnish).[14] However, the fact remains that, regardless of the orthography, any suggestion that proficiency in one's *first* alphabetic writing system (ancient or modern) can be achieved in a few days or weeks must be considered most problematic.[15] Thus any argument about widespread

14. "Deep orthography" and "shallow orthography" are technical terms used in the descriptions of alphabetic systems (Seymour 2005; Gough, Juel, and Griffith 1992). A "deep orthography" is a system in which there is not a "simple correspondence" between letters and sounds, and complexities and irregularities are quite common. Along these lines, Ehri has stated,

> according to our theory, graphemes that do not follow the conventional system in symbolizing phonemes should be harder to store in representations than graphemes conforming to the system. Also, phonemes having many graphemic options should be a bigger burden on memory than phonemes having only a couple of options. In addition, graphemes that have no correlates in sound, for example, doubled letters and silent letters, should elude memory. Likewise, spelling patterns that recur in few other words [and] are not built out of conventional graphemes and phonemes should cause problems. (Ehri 1997: 248; see also Treiman 1993)

Because German orthography is a shallow(er) orthography, proficiency can be more rapidly achieved. Indeed, Wimmer and Landerl have suggested that eight or nine months are often sufficient for basic proficiency, but they also candidly affirm that certain aspects of German orthography (for example, consonantal clusters) can present continuing difficulties (Wimmer and Landerl 1997: 89–91 and passim). Because French has a deep orthography, with many written markers that are not reflected in pronunciation, proficiency in the French writing system normally requires years (Totereau, Thevenin, and Fayol 1997).

Note that proponents of the "Script Dependent Hypothesis" affirm that some children may have substantial difficulties learning a writing system with a deep orthography but minimal difficulties learning a writing system with a shallow orthography. Proponents of the "Central Processing Hypothesis" affirm that children having difficulties with the learning of a writing system with a deep orthography will also normally have similar problems learning a writing system for a shallow orthography. Recently, some have suggested that the Central Processing Hypothesis and Script Dependent Hypothesis may be complementary (Geva 1995).

15. Of course, because of the dominance of consonants in the Hebrew writing system, some might suggest that becoming proficient in the ancient Hebrew (or Phoenician, or Aramaic) writing system was accomplished with particular ease and at a rapid pace. Of import is the fact that some studies of proficiency in the modern Hebrew writing system (as one's first writing system) have been produced and are, for this essay, among the most relevant of all the studies of the development of proficiency in modern writing systems. Levin (personal correspondence) has

literacy that is based on the "ease of learning one's first alphabet" must be considered problematic.

Alphabets and Literacy: Observations and Animadversions

Some scholars might still believe that high rates of literacy are a necessary corollary of alphabetic writing, and higher rates of literacy must be posited as existing for alphabetic societies in antiquity (including the Iron Age Levant). However, the data do not support the contention that a high rate of literacy is a necessary corollary of a society with an alphabetic writing system. (1) For example, Greek is an alphabetic script (derived from the Phoenician script), but there is no decisive evidence that literacy of the populace in ancient Greece was the norm. (2) Moreover, Latin is an alphabetic script as well, but there is no decisive evidence that literacy was

---

summarized the progression of facility in the modern Hebrew writing system as follows: (1) Israeli children begin writing words phonetically at around five years of age. (2) Training in the basic features of orthography, including Masoretic pointing, continues for most children through the age of eight. (3) Most spelling errors disappear by around the age of ten, but some (for example, the usage of *yod* and *waw* as *matres lectionis*) persist into adulthood even among literate adults (see also Share and Levin 1999; Levin, Share, and Shatil 1996; Ravid 1995). In short, multiple years are normally necessary for proficiency. Of course, there are certain aspects of modern Hebrew phonology and orthography that differ from ancient Hebrew (see Berent and Frost 1997), but I do not believe that this factor would result in grossly disproportionate differences in the time required for proficiency.

Some might suggest that adult Olim can learn to reproduce the script in a matter of hours and that this is demonstrative of the fact that the linear alphabetic script is so simple that almost no instruction is needed (in antiquity or in the modern period). The problem with this analogy is that adult Olim already have the cognitive building blocks and the manual dexterity in place, established previously, when they learned their first writing system. For this reason, any comparison between modern adult Olim and ancient Israelites learning their *first* writing system is fundamentally flawed.

With regard to Arabic, Assaad Skaff and Helen Sader (personal correspondence) have noted that the short vowels and the long vowels are learned at the same time, along with the consonants. This training begins in earnest during the first grade (although parents often begin instruction in the home at an earlier age). During the succeeding years, proficiency begins to develop, and by the ninth grade ("brevet" according to French nomenclature) students are very capable of writing Arabic with substantial proficiency. Thus the learning of Arabic parallels, in many respects, the pace of learning modern Hebrew in Israel. In short, becoming proficient in writing and reading one's first language in a linear alphabetic script (such as would be the case with children learning to write their native language) is not a process that can be considered simple.

the norm for the populace in ancient Italy. Rather, the evidence suggests that the vast majority of the population was not literate.[16] (3) Similar statements can be made for the European world of the Middle Ages. (4) Furthermore, some societies or regions with complex nonalphabetic writing systems have very high literacy rates, but some with alphabetic writing systems have low literacy rates. Obviously, this is the case for China and Japan. I am not suggesting that there is no relationship between the complexity of a writing system and literacy rates. Rather, I am suggesting that there were multiple variables and that the nature of the writing system is simply one of these variables – and not even the most determinative variable.[17] Ultimately, writing systems and literacy rates are related but independent variables. Thus the supposition that widespread literacy across socioeconomic boundaries is a necessary correlative of the use of the alphabet should be considered dubious.

Abecedaries: Aegis and Function

It is not possible to determine the precise aegis (palace or temple, etc.) for the Tel Zayit Abecedary or the non-aegis (some sort of quasi-independent scribal guild) for this inscription. Recently, there has been substantive discussion about factors of this sort for epigraphs from Iron I and Iron II (Sanders 2004; R. Byrne 2007; van der Toorn 2007). Nevertheless, we must concede that for the Tel Zayit Abecedary the Sitz im Leben of its production is not known. After all, the Tel Zayit Abecedary was found in a secondary or tertiary context, not a primary context (Tappy et al. 2006: 6). Furthermore, there were no accompanying inscriptions found in the same locus. Finding an inscription in a primary context often permits some discussion about aegis and reason for production.

Furthermore, associated epigraphs often provide data that are complementary (for interpretive purposes). However, with the Tel Zayit Abecedary, these sorts of data are not available; therefore, the discernment of its original raison d'être is especially difficult. Someone might suggest that all abecedaries must have functioned in instructional contexts, thus requiring that there was a school at Tel Zayit. Remember, however, that Lemaire (1981) has been subjected to severe criticism for his proposal that the presence of an abecedary at an archaeological site is demonstrative of the

16. W. V. Harris has suggested that literacy rates in Attica were probably about 5–10 percent, and rates in Italy were probably below 15 percent (see Harris 1989: 22, 114, 267). Within this volume (passim), Harris has cogently criticized scholars who have proposed high(er) rates of literacy for the populace. See especially his analyses of E. A. Havelock 1982 and A. M. Guillemin 1937.

17. On some of the determinative variables, see W. V. Harris 1989: 12–24.

presence of an ancient school at a site (for example, Haran 1988; Crenshaw 1985: 605–7; 1998: 100–108; Weeks 1994: 132–56; see also Puech 1988). Striking is the fact that even within the *editio princeps* of the Tel Zayit Abecedary, possible mantic functions are apparently foregrounded to some extent (Tappy et al. 2006: 42). My own position is that one can hardly suggest that none of the extant abecedaries is to be associated with curricular activities (Rollston 2006: 67). However, based on the current extant epigraphic data, it is difficult to say more than this about the nature and function of abecedaries.

Nevertheless, I hasten to add that this ambiguity must not be construed as suggesting that the Tel Zayit Abecedary is unimportant. On the contrary, I believe that it is an important piece of the literacy puzzle. That is, from this inscription we can affirm that someone at Zayit was writing. (In other words, I do not think it probable that this stone was brought to the site after it was inscribed.) Arguably, the inscription was Judean (based on Tappy's arguments about Tel Zayit's being a Judean site in this period of its history). Furthermore, the inscriber of the Tel Zayit Abecedary was probably not the only literate person at Zayit in this chronological horizon. Moreover, this inscription is demonstrably early – in my opinion, late 10th century or very early 9th century B.C.E. – so it joins a rare and elite group of inscriptions from the southern Levant. Moreover, because it was found in a secure archaeological context (that is, not purchased from the market and not a surface find), it will continue to factor in discussions in important ways. Of course, it would have been more helpful if it had been found in a primary context, but it was not. In sum, the Tel Zayit Abecedary is indeed an important piece of the puzzle. Nevertheless, there are not enough pieces of this puzzle to understand in a precise fashion just how the Tel Zayit inscription figures into the entirety. Caution, therefore, must be the epigrapher's modus operandi.

The Iron Age Phoenician Script: General Introduction

To date, there has been substantial discussion about the script series to which the Tel Zayit Abecedary belongs. Before focusing on the script series of the Tel Zayit Abecedary, I must refer to some of the history of the development of the Iron Age national scripts. (1) Within the field of Iron Age Northwest Semitic paleography, the consensus has long been that the Iron Age Phoenician script descended from the early alphabetic script of the Middle Bronze and Late Bronze Ages (see Darnell 2005). (2) During the Iron Age, the Phoenician script continued to be used. Indeed, for some time it was the international prestige script of the Levant. The Phoe-

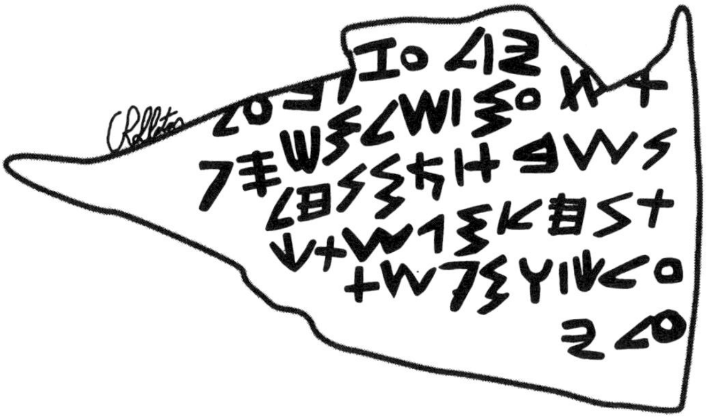

Fig. 2. Bronze ʿAzarbaʿl inscription. (Drawing by Christopher Rollston)

nician script is attested not only in Phoenicia but also in various (other) regions of the ancient Near East and Mediterranean (because, for example, of Phoenician colonization in certain regions and general cultural influence in other regions). This script has been the subject of substantive analyses (Peckham 1968; McCarter 1975). (3) Nevertheless, during the Iron Age certain daughter scripts developed from the Phoenician *Mutterschrift* (and became independent national scripts). Among the most important are the Old Hebrew script and the Aramaic script. These script series have also been the subject of substantive analyses.[18] (4) For the Phoenician, Old Hebrew, and Aramaic scripts, there are distinguishing diagnostic features; Northwest Semitic paleographers have often focused on elucidating them (Naveh 1987: 89–100; Rollston 2006: 58–61; forthcoming b).

The Phoenician Mutterschrift *in the Homeland*

There are a number of Phoenician inscriptions from the Phoenician homeland itself that provide substantial data about the Phoenician script of the late 11th, 10th, and early 9th centuries. Among the most important of the early Phoenician inscriptions is the Bronze ʿAzarbaʿl Inscription

18. Naveh 1970 (Aramaic); Cross 1961; 1962a; 1962b (Old Hebrew); Naveh 1987 (Phoenician, Old Hebrew, Aramaic, etc.); Rollston 1999; 2003; 2006 (Old Hebrew).

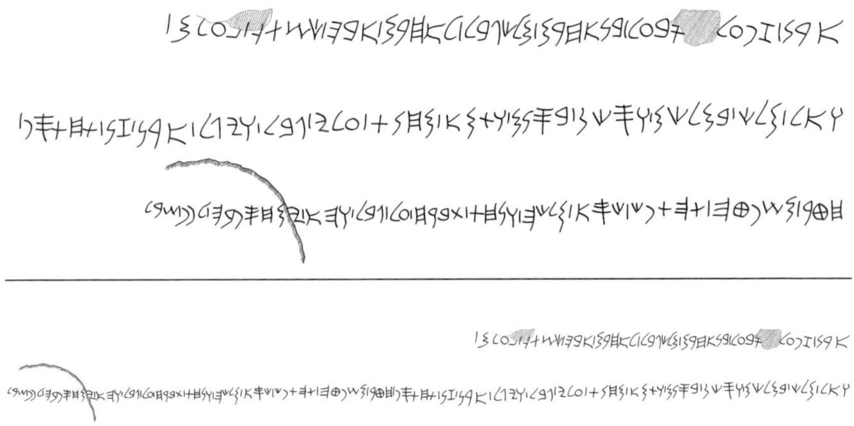

Fig. 3. Drawing of ʾAḥiram inscription by Marilyn Lundberg. Above: line-by-line transcription (Line 1 = Side 1; Lines 2–3 = Side 2). Below: transcription with Side in a single line (Line 1 = Side 1; Line 2 + Side 2). Used by permission.

(often referred to as the Bronze Spatula Inscription). This prestige object was discovered during controlled excavations at Byblos (ancient Gebal). Six lines of Phoenician text (often considered enigmatic) are etched into the metal. The script reflects archaic features, such as the trident *kap*, the *mem* with a strong vertical stance (and without the lengthening of the fifth stroke), truncated vertical shaft of *samek*, and the box-shaped *ḥet*. Some have argued that this inscription reflects the terminal horizon of the 11th century, but a date in the (early) 10th century is also tenable.

There are several 10th-century "Royal Phoenician inscriptions" from Byblos. Among the most impressive is the ʾAḥiram Sarcophagus Inscription, an inscription that was commissioned by ʾAḥiram's son ʾIttobaʿl. The majority of this inscription is written on the lid of the sarcophagus (the length of it), but the initial component of the inscription is written on the end of the sarcophagus itself (that is, not on the lid). Most of the letters were chiseled with care and substantial precision, although there is a diminution of letter size that is visible (and quantifiable) in the terminal portions of the inscription. The Phoenician script of the ʾAḥiram Sarcophagus is distinguishable from the script of the ʿAzarbaʿl Inscription; that is, some typological developments are present. Among the most important developments are the distinct lengthening of the vertical shaft of *samek*, the lengthening of the fifth stroke of *mem*, and the lengthening of the verticals of *ḥet*.

Fig. 4. Shipiṭbaʿl inscription.

Hailing also from Byblos during the same basic horizon are the Yeḥimilk Inscription, the ʾAbibaʿl Inscription and the ʾElibaʿl Inscription. Yeḥimilk is a monumental inscription, chiseled into a stone tablet. The ʾAbibaʿl Inscription is inscribed on a statue of Pharaoh Sheshonk I (reigned ca. 945–924 B.C.E.) and thus figures among the most interesting and important of the early Byblian lapidary inscriptions. Similarly, the inscription of ʾElibaʿl was written on a bust of Pharaoh Osorkon I (reigned ca. 924–889 B.C.E.). Also of consequence is the fact that within this inscription ʾElibaʿl provides his father's name: Yeḥi[milk]. I argue that the inscriptions of Yeḥimilk, ʾAbibaʿl, and ʾElibaʿl reflect the same basic script typology as the typology of the ʾAḥiram Sarcophagus Inscription. To be sure, some modest typological differences have been discussed, but the most important facts are that these Phoenician inscriptions all reflect the same basic script morphology and all are royal ("King of Byblos" being the most dominant referential feature of these monumental inscriptions).

The inscription of Shipiṭbaʿl is often classed as the final of the great Old Byblian (Phoenician) inscriptions of this horizon (see also the ʿAbdaʾ Sherd Graffito from this horizon). One aspect of the Shipiṭbaʿl Inscription that has garnered much discussion is the presence of a three-generation genealogy: Shipiṭbaʿl, king of Byblos; son of ʾElibaʿl, king of Byblos; son of Yeḥimilk, king of Byblos. Significantly, the script of the Shipiṭbaʿl Inscription contains features that reflect typological development (that is, when compared with the script of ʾAḥiram, Yeḥimilk, ʾAbibaʿl, and ʾElibaʿl). For example, the fifth stroke of *mem* is beginning to elongate more, and some incipient rotation of the fledgling "head" has begun; similar trends are apparent in *nun*. The main point, however, is that during this horizon the Phoenician script reflects a standardized script and attention to accepted ancient morphology and ductus. Moreover, some modest development is also attested in the latest of the Old Byblian inscriptions, a predictable and important aspect of this cohesive corpus.

Based on the convergence of paleographic data, prosopographic data, and the synchronisms (with the Egyptian kings), the following is often posited: (1) Yeḥimilk was the father of ʾElibaʿl, and ʾElibaʿl was the father of Shipiṭbaʿl. (2) Because the script of the ʾAḥiram Sarcophagus is typologically earlier than the script of Shipiṭbaʿl, some argue that the reigns of the Byblian kings ʾAḥiram and his son ʾIttobaʿl were earlier than the reigns of Yeḥimilk, ʾElibaʿl, and Shipiṭbaʿl. (3) Because the inscription of ʾAbibaʿl is engraved into a statue of Sheshonk I (reigned ca. 945–924 B.C.E.) and because the inscription of ʾElibaʿl is engraved into a bust of Osorkon I (reigned ca. 924–889 B.C.E.), some argue that the reign of ʾAbibaʿl preceded ʾElibaʿl's. Note that some epigraphers posit that ʾAbibaʿl and ʾElibaʿl were brothers. Of course, this hypothesis results in the placement of the reigns of ʾAḥiram and ʾIttobaʿl at the beginning of the sequence. The final sequence is arranged as follows: ʾAḥiram, ʾIttobaʿl, Yeḥimilk, ʾAbibaʿl, ʾElibaʿl, Shipiṭbaʿl.[19]

Nevertheless, the precise regnal sequence is not a fundamental point for this essay. Rather, the fundamental points are: (1) These Phoenician inscriptions from Byblos reflect substantial script continuity with discernible typological development: the ʿAzarbaʿl Inscription is the most archaic script, the script of the ʾAḥiram Sarcophagus, Yeḥimilk, ʾAbibaʿl, and ʾElibaʿl is more typologically advanced than that of ʿAzarbaʿl, and the script of Shipiṭbaʿl is the most developed typologically. (2) The fact that two of these inscriptions are engraved on stones with the names of Sheshonk I and Osorkon I functions as an important control, useful as a historical peg for discussions of absolute dates. That is, the data converge to demonstrate beyond a reasonable doubt that these royal Phoenician inscriptions hail from Byblos during the 10th and early 9th centuries. At this point, I should also emphasize that recent attempts to lower the chronology of these Byblian inscriptions to the mid-9th and mid-8th centuries are, for numerous reasons, untenable.[20]

19. See also the discussion in Donner and Röllig 1979: 2.2–10.

20. Sass has proposed a dramatic lowering of these dates (see Sass 2005). However, his proposal is plagued with serious paleographic and historical problems; therefore, his attempt to compress the dates is not at all tenable. I shall turn to these problems in a subsequent publication.

Fig. 5. Nora Stone. (Drawing by Christopher Rollston)

The Iron Age Phoenician Script: International Usage

Because of Phoenician colonization and seafaring, the Phoenician script (and often language) began to be employed in numerous regions (not only in regions such as Byblos, Tyre, and Sidon). For example, from Cyprus comes the Honeyman Inscription, a monumental Phoenician inscription from the 9th century. The Nora Inscription was found on the Mediterranean island of Sardinia and can be dated with substantial certitude to the (late) 9th century. The Kition Bowl was found at Kition (Cyprus) and reflects a fine Phoenician cursive of the mid-8th century. Moreover, the Seville Statuette (Spain) dates to the second half of the 8th century and employs the Phoenician script. Additionally, the Malta Stele, from the late 8th century, reflects a fine Phoenician script. One of the most important of the Phoenician inscriptions from the (late) 8th century is the Karatepe Inscription (Asia Minor). Within this inscription, the Anatolian (Neo-Hittite) regent Azitawadda also commissioned a Phoenician inscription (8th century) to parallel his (native) Hittite hieroglyphic rendition. This inscription (from the site of Karatepe) is the longest of the Phoenician inscriptions (see McCarter 1975; Peckham 1968). The point is that

Fig. 6. Kefar Veradim inscribed bowl. (Drawing by Christopher Rollston)

the Phoenician script became a dominant Northwest Semitic script tradition during the 10th, 9th, and 8th centuries. Moreover, lapidary and cursive inscriptions are attested from regions near to and far from the Phoenician homeland.

Nevertheless, these are not the sole cases of the transregional use of the Phoenician script. For example, the late-9th-century Kilamuwa Inscription is written in the Phoenician language (rather than the local dialect) and (arguably) the Phoenician script – that is, the prestige script and language of this chronological horizon. Also of import is the fact that for a time texts written in the Aramaic language continued to use the Phoenician script. For example, the Tell Fakhariyeh Statue Bilingual Inscription (9th century) employs the Phoenician script for the Aramaic text. The Hadad and Panamuwa Inscriptions from Samʾal (all 8th century) are written in an Aramaic dialect but employ the Phoenician script. Moreover, the Bar-Rakib Inscription is written in the standard Old Aramaic dialect, but the script continues to be the Phoenician script (see Naveh 1987: 79–80).[21] Of course, a distinctive Aramaic script did develop (beginning in the 9th century, fully developed in the 8th century B.C.E.), but it is significant that the Phoenician script (considered a "classical prestige script") had been used for many inscriptions written in the Aramaic language (so Naveh 1970; 1987). That is, the Phoenician script (and even language, at times) was an international, transregional script.

Among the most important inscriptions is the inscribed bronze bowl from Kefar Veradim, a prestige item of very high quality from a tomb in the Galilee (see Alexandre 2006). The script of this inscription is stun-

21. Note that there are some differences between Naveh and Cross on the development of the Aramaic script. For more on these differences, see below.

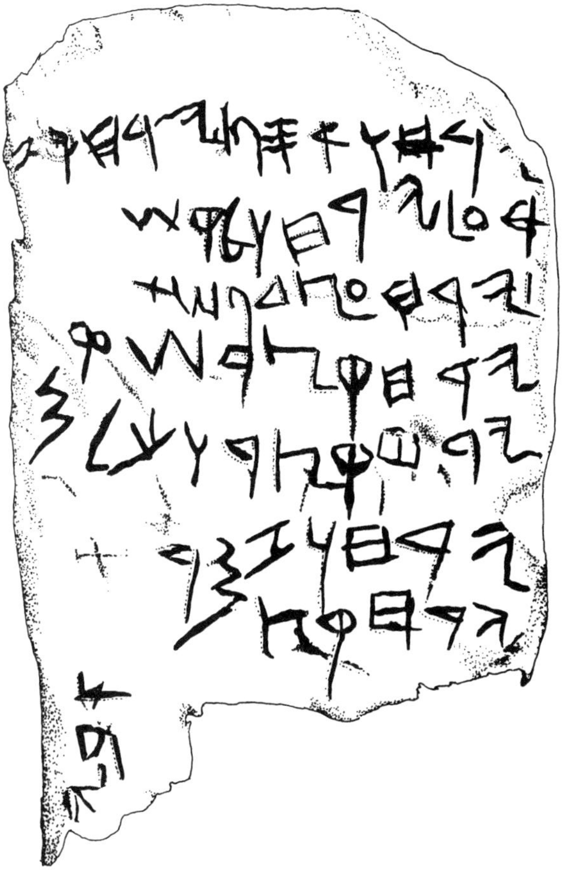

Fig. 7. Drawing of the Gezer Calendar.

ning, reflecting the consummate work of a fine engraver. Also significant is the fact that its script reflects the same basic script morphology as the ʿAzarbaʿl Inscription. For example, *kap* is trident-shaped, *samek* has a "truncated" vertical shaft, and the *ḥet* is box-shaped. There can be no question about the fact that this inscription is written in the Phoenician script. In fact, it is a superb Phoenician script, and of fundamental importance is the fact that it was discovered in Israel. That is, the Phoenician script is attested in Israel, and this fact cannot be contested.

During Macalister's excavations in 1908, a small limestone "tablet" was discovered in debris from his "Fourth Semitic" period – a period that Albright associated with Iron I (see Macalister 1908; Albright 1943). Because the contents of the inscription revolve around seasonal agricultural activities (for example, sowing, harvesting, and processing of flax and barley), the tablet is often considered to be some sort of an agricultural "calendar." Naveh has argued that "the script of the Gezer Calendar, thought to be the earliest Hebrew inscription known to date, resembles the writing of the tenth-century B.C. Phoenician inscriptions from Byblos." He then goes on to state that "at this stage no specifically Hebrew characters can be distinguished, and the Hebrew followed the scribal tradition current in Canaan" (Naveh 1987: 65).

I have collated various Phoenician inscriptions from Lebanon, and I concur with Naveh's assessment. That is, I do not think the script of the Gezer Calendar exhibits diagnostic features (for example, letter morphology, stance, pronounced curvature) that would suggest it should be classified as the Old Hebrew script. I consider the script of the Gezer Calendar to be Phoenician. Regarding this script, I note that certain basic features (for example, the *waw*) are typologically later than the Old Byblian inscriptions and also typologically later than the script of the Tel Zayit Abecedary. However, certain features of the script of the Gezer Calendar are typologically earlier. For example, the *mem* of the Gezer Calendar is typologically earlier than the *mem* of the Tel Zayit inscription; but note that it is quite similar to the *mem* of the Shipiṭbaʿl Inscription, among the latest of the Old Byblian inscriptions.

Also note that Cross considers the Gezer Calendar to be written in the Hebrew language (Cross and Freedman 1952: 46–47). Regarding the script of the Gezer Calendar, Cross has written, "so similar are Phoenician and Hebrew in the tenth century that it has been difficult for epigraphists to establish whether the Gezer Calendar was written in a Hebrew or in a Phoenician script." Cross continues by stating, "I believe that the first rudimentary innovations that will mark the emergent Hebrew script can be perceived in the Gezer Calendar, but they are faint at best." He then affirms that "these rudimentary features include the elongation of the vertical strokes or legs of such letters as *ʾalep, waw, kap, mem,* and *reš*." To be sure, the differences between Naveh and Cross are modest. Moreover, Cross even concedes that the features which distinguish the fledgling Old Hebrew script from the Phoenician *Mutterschrift* are "faint at best" (Cross 1980; 2003: 226).

Reference should be made to some early inscriptions that have been found in Israel, for example, the inscriptions found at Hazor Stratum IX and Stratum VIII. Although they are fragmentary, I suggest it is readily ap-

Fig. 8. Drawing of the Tel Zayit abecedary by P. Kyle McCarter Jr.

parent that none of these inscriptions reflects paleographic features that are demonstrative of the Old Hebrew script. In other words, they contain nothing that is diagnostic of Old Hebrew. Similar statements can be made about the (fragmentary) inscriptions from Khirbet Roš Zayit, Beth-shemesh, and Tel Batash (Timnah).[22] Of course, some of the Arad ostraca are affirmed to have come from horizons antecedent to the 9th century (Aharoni 1981). Some of these ostraca are indeed early; however, the inscriptions from these early strata are faded, abraded, and fragmentary and thus are precarious bases for definitive statements about the script. The main point is that there are inscriptions written in the Phoenician script that are attested at various geographical sites.

The Script Series of the Tel Zayit Abecedary

The Tel Zayit Abecedary hails from an archaeological context that Tappy considers to be the 10th century (Tappy et al. 2006: 5–25). The inscription was carved into a stone. Although the second half is quite

22. For these inscriptions, see Yadin et al. 1960: 70–75 and plates; Yadin et al. 1961: esp. 346–47; Gal 1990; Bunimovitz and Lederman 1997; Kelm and Mazar 1995: 111; Mazar 2003.

abraded, it is certain that this abecedary is complete. The script reflects typological developments not attested in the Kefar Veradim Bowl Inscription, ʿAzarbaʿl Inscription, or ʾAḥiram, Yeḥimilk, ʾAbibaʿl, and ʾElibaʿl Inscriptions.

For example, *kap* is not trident-shaped but, rather, has begun to develop a leg. (Note that even Shipiṭbaʿl retains the trident-shaped *kap*.) Moreover, the fifth stroke of *mem* and the third stroke of *nun* have begun to elongate. In addition, the entire letter has begun to rotate. These sorts of typological features reflect the fact that the Tel Zayit Abecedary is typologically later than the Old Byblian inscriptions and the Kefar Veradim Bowl Inscription.

To be sure, there are a modest number of features of the Tel Zayit Abecedary that are typologically earlier. Among the most significant of these is the *waw*. Of course, preservations of typologically older forms are to be anticipated at times in inscriptions. Based on the paleographic data, I argue that this inscription can be dated to the late 10th century or the very early 9th century (that is, I date it slightly later than Tappy wishes to date the archaeological context). Based on the paleographic data, I believe that the Tel Zayit Abecedary constitutes a nice example of the use of the Phoenician script in Iron Age Israel. Moreover, based on the convergence of paleographic data, I argue that the Tel Zayit Abecedary and the Gezer Calendar hail from the same basic chronological horizon.[23]

Regarding the script series, McCarter has argued in the editio princeps of the Tel Zayit Abecedary that its script is not Phoenician but a distinct South Canaanite script derived from the Phoenician script.[24] Moreover, this South Canaanite script is affirmed to be a transitional script that "in the tenth century . . . [it] already exhibits characteristics that anticipate the distinctive features of the mature Hebrew national script" (Tappy et al.

23. Of course, it is imperative to note that certain aspects of the Gezer Calendar are often argued to be indicative of the hand of a fledgling student. This position may be tenable, but the fact remains that the letter forms reflect important typological features. Similar statements can be made about the Tel Zayit Abecedary.

24. There is another factor that must be mentioned as well: the Tel Zayit Abecedary preserves a single example of each letter (and some of these are not well preserved!). Moreover, for the Phoenician series of the 10th and 9th centuries, we have modest numbers of inscriptions. Thus I urge caution in attempting to argue that this inscription differs from the Phoenician series in this or that fashion. Furthermore, I shall argue that there are no non-Phoenician script features in the Tel Zayit Abecedary. That is, I respectfully differ with Kyle McCarter, my beloved *Doktorvater*, mentor, and friend. My hope is that, in some fashion, the fact that I do differ is viewed as a tribute to the scholar from whom I have learned most and best.

2006: 26, 28). This development is considered to be "a major watershed in the evolution of alphabetic writing in southern Canaan at the outset of Iron Age IIA, and the principal result of this phenomenon emerged as the mature Hebrew national script of the first millennium" (Tappy et al. 2006: 42 and passim). Thus within the *editio princeps*, it is affirmed that the script of the Tel Zayit Abecedary is not that of the Phoenician script series, but rather is basically a nascent Old Hebrew script. Moreover, it is also argued that similar statements can be made about the (fragmentary) inscriptions from sites such as Beth-shemesh, Tel ʿAmal, Tel Batash, and Tel Reḥov (Tappy et al. 2006: 28).

Note, however, that the Beth-shemesh Inscription consists of only three discernible letters (*ḥnn*), the inscription from ʿAmal consists of only four letters (*lnmš*), the inscription from Batash consists of only four letters (*nḥnn*), and the inscription from Reḥov consists of three preserved letters (*lnḥ*). Obviously, these data are brief and the inscriptions are fragmentary and often abraded as well. Moreover, I posit that there are no features in these inscriptions that must be considered non-Phoenician. I also believe that the same can be said of the brief and fragmentary inscriptions from Roš Zayit, Tell el Faraʿ (South), and ʾEshtemoaʿ.

McCarter's position regarding the script of the Tel Zayit Abecedary is important and nuanced. Nonetheless, I must respectfully disagree. That is, I argue that the script of the Tel Zayit Abecedary fits nicely within the Phoenician script series. A major component of McCarter's argument that this is not the Phoenician script is the contention that elongation is not a feature of the Phoenician script. To be precise, it is affirmed that "the elongation of *ʾalep*, *he*, *waw*, *kap*, *mem*, *nun*, and *reš*" argues against considering it to be Phoenician and is evidence for the fact that it is a transitional script that anticipates the distinctive "features of the mature Hebrew national script." Furthermore, it is argued that this resistance of elongation is "underscored by the persistence into the ninth century of a preference for compact, well-proportioned characters of the kind seen, for example, in maritime Phoenician inscriptions such as the so-called Honeyman inscriptions from Cyprus and the *taršiš* inscription from Nora in Sardinia" (Tappy et al. 2006: 30).

However, I do not consider elongation to be a distinctive marker of a particular script series. My reason for this view is as follows: *the Phoenician, Aramaic, and Old Hebrew script series all reflect elongation.*

For example, (1) note that the relative length of the vertical stroke of the *ʾalep* in the Tell Fakhariyeh Inscription is as long as in the *ʾalep* of Tel Zayit (and all agree that the script of the Tell Fakhariyeh is Phoenician and early). Moreover, there is more elongation in the *ʾalep* of the Bir-Hadad Inscription than there is in the Tel Zayit Abecedary.

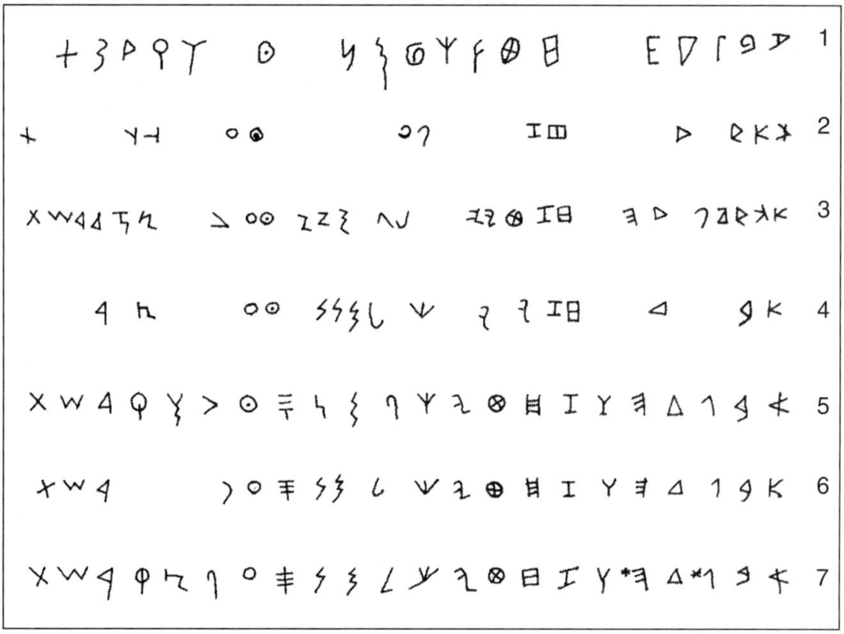

Early Phoenician Scripts

Line 1. From the ʿIzbet Ṣarṭah Ostracon of ca. 1100 B.C.E.
Line 2. From the ʾEl-Ḫaḍr Arrowheads of the early 11th century B.C.E.
Line 3. From inscribed arrowheads of the mid-11th century B.C.E.
Line 4. From inscribed arrowheads of the late 11th century B.C.E.
Line 5. From the Tell Faḫariyeh Inscription.
Line 6. From the ʾAḥiram Inscription of ca. 1000–975 B.C.E.
Line 7. From the Gezer Calendar of the 10th century B.C.E.

Fig. 9. Cross's chart of Early Phoenician scripts. From F. M. Cross, Leaves from an Leaves from an Epigrapher's Notebook: Collected Papers in Hebrew and West Semitic Palaeography and Epigraphy *(HSS 51; Winona Lake, IN: Eisenbrauns, 2003) fig. 4.2, p. 55. Used by permission.*

(2) Regarding the *he*, similar statements can be made. Note that the vertical stroke of *he* in the Tell Fakhariyeh Inscription reflects elongation, even though this Phoenician script is early. Note too that in the Bir-Hadad Inscription, the *he* is also elongated. The same is true for the Kilamuwa Inscription and also for the ʿAmman Citadel Inscription.

(3) The *waw* of the Tell Fakhariyeh Inscription reflects elongation as well. Moreover, the same is true of the *waw* of the Bir-Hadad Inscription

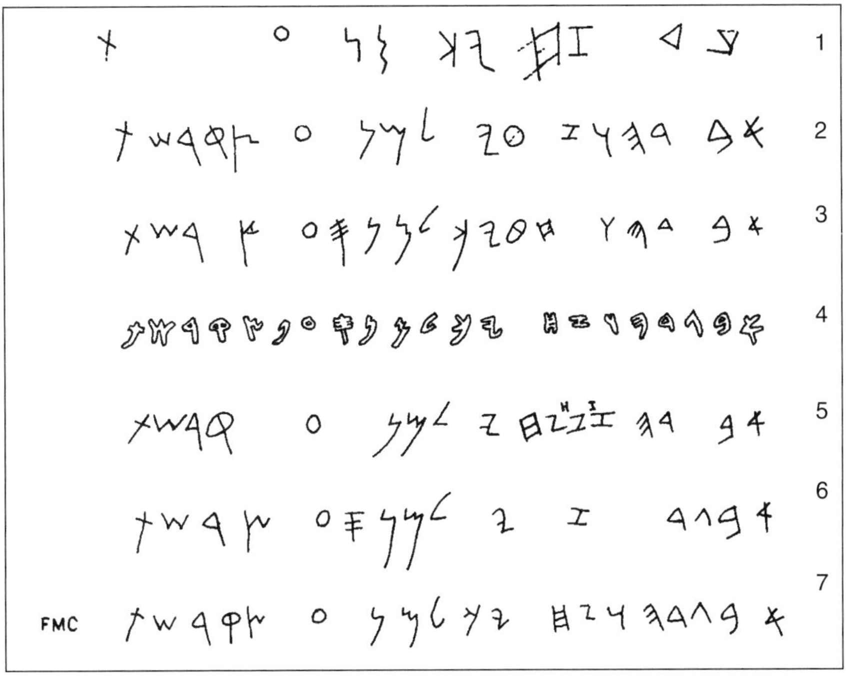

Early Aramaic Scripts

Line 1. From the Gozan Pedestal Inscription of ca. 900 B.C.E.
Line 2. From the Ben Hadad Inscription of ca. 850 B.C.E.
Line 3. From the ʿAmman Citadel Inscription of the mid-9th century B.C.E.
Line 4. From the Kilamuwa Inscription of ca. 825 B.C.E.
Line 5. From the Ḥazaʾel Inscriptions (H = Horse Ornament; I = Ivory) of ca. 825 B.C.E.
Line 6. From the Luristan Bronze Jug of ca. 800 B.C.E.
Line 7. From the Zakkur Inscription of ca. 800–775 B.C.E.

Fig. 10. Cross's chart of Early Phoenician scripts. From F. M. Cross, Leaves from an Leaves from an Epigrapher's Notebook: Collected Papers in Hebrew and West Semitic Palaeography and Epigraphy *(HSS 51; Winona Lake, IN: Eisenbrauns, 2003) fig. 4.3, p. 59. Used by permission.*

and the ʿAmman Citadel Inscription. (4) It is again critical to note that in the Tell Fakhariyeh Inscription, the *kap* reflects some elongation (that is, it is no longer just the trident). Within the ʿAmman Citadel Inscription, there is substantial elongation of the *kap*. Furthermore, and of fundamental importance, note that there is some significant elongation in the

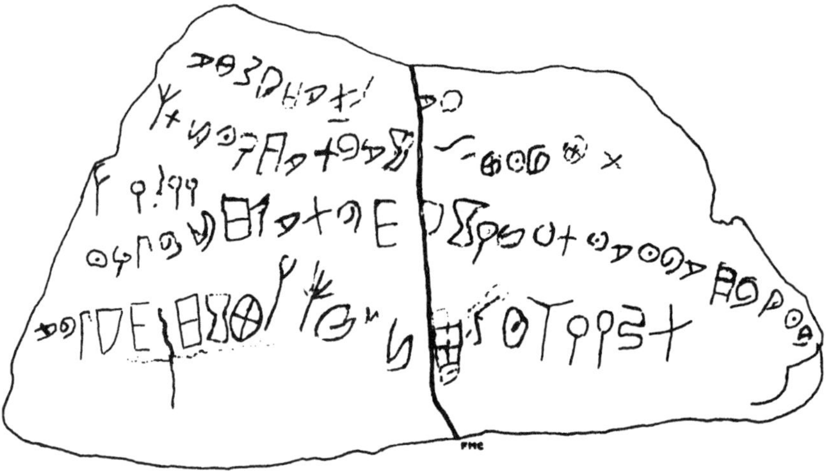

Fig. 11. ʿIzbet Ṣarṭah Ostracon. Drawing by F. M. Cross, Leaves from an Leaves from an Epigrapher's Notebook: Collected Papers in Hebrew and West Semitic Palaeography and Epigraphy *(HSS 51; Winona Lake, IN: Eisenbrauns, 2003) fig. 32.6, p. 221. Used by permission.*

Phoenician ostracon from ʿIzbet Ṣarṭah, normally dated to the 11th century B.C.E.! (5) Notice also the pronounced elongation present in the Phoenician script of subsequent centuries, as revealed in the 8th-century Kition Bowl. Again, then, it would be difficult to suggest that elongation is a distinctive feature of Old Hebrew, nascent Old Hebrew, or transitional South Canaanite scripts.

(6) Regarding the *mem* and *nun*, note that there is some elongation that occurs in the ʾAḥiram Sarcophagus Inscription. Furthermore, there is also substantial elongation of both of these letters in the Bir-Hadad Inscription, Kilamuwa Inscription, and Shipiṭbaʿl Inscription. Obviously, these data militate very strongly against suggesting that elongation of these letters in the Tel Zayit Abecedary should be considered a non-Phoenician, nascent Old Hebrew feature. (7) Furthermore, regarding the *reš*, the same observations can be made. Elongation of this letter is pronounced, for example, in the Bir-Hadad Inscription and the ʿAmman Citadel Inscription.

Someone might counter by suggesting that some of this elongation is attested in the Aramaic series and thus is not relevant in a discussion of the Phoenician series. (1) I note, however, that Naveh (differing with Cross) has argued that the Aramaic national script "begins roughly in the mid-eighth century B.C." (Naveh 1970 passim; 1987: 80). Thus Naveh

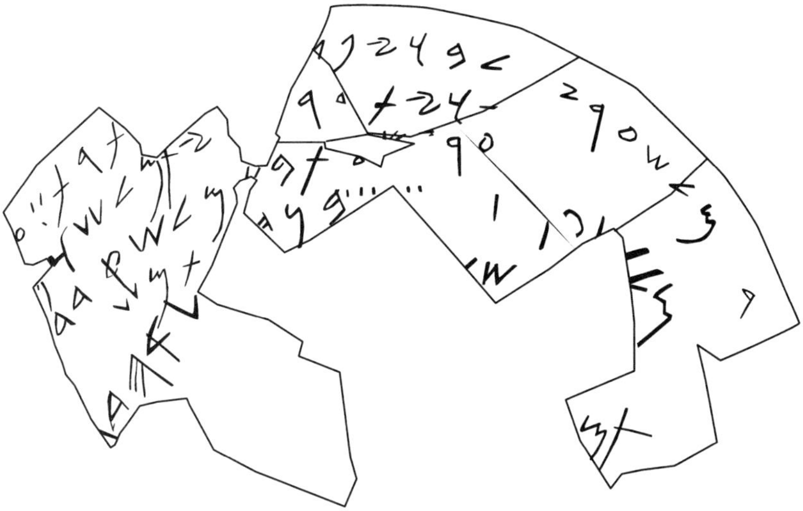

Fig. 12. Kition Bowl. (Drawing by Christopher Rollston)

would ostensibly argue that inscriptions such as the Gozan Pedestal Inscription, the Bir-Hadad Inscription, the Haza'el Inscriptions, the ʿAmman Citadel Inscription, and the Kilamuwa Inscription were written in the Phoenician script. (2) Moreover, and of critical importance, even if one concurs with Cross (against Naveh) on his assignment of certain 10th- and 9th-century inscriptions to the Aramaic series, the fact remains that elongation is present even in some of the inscriptions that all paleographers agree are written in the Phoenician script. (3) Some might retort that it is unacceptable to use the script of the Tell Fakhariyeh Inscription in this discussion. However, I would counter that it would be imprudent to ignore or "factor out" the data from Tell Fakhariyeh. After all, Cross has argued that it represents the Phoenician script, and although the text dates to the 9th century B.C.E., he has stated that the script "falls in the typological sequence among inscriptions of the end of the eleventh or the beginning of the tenth century B.C.E." That is, he considers the script to be Phoenician and considers it to be reflective of the late 11th or early 10th century B.C.E. (Cross 1995: 408; cf. also Naveh 1987: 101–13).[25] Thus, regardless

25. Note that Cross does not think Fakhariyeh shows much tendency "to lengthen final downstrokes" (Cross 1995: 407). Nonetheless, I note that even his drawings reveal some significant lengthening of some of the downstrokes in this inscription.

of its actual date of composition, Cross and Naveh have agreed that its script is Phoenician, and they have agreed that the script is typologically the Phoenician script of the 10th century B.C.E. Hence it is directly relevant to a comparative assessment of the Tel Zayit Abecedary.

Regarding the script series of the Tel Zayit inscription, I should like to make several further observations. (1) McCarter has stated that the head of *bet* in the Tel Zayit Abecedary is "rounded and larger than the usually triangular *bet* of the contemporary Phoenician parent script as represented by the Byblian series" (Tappy et al. 2006: 32). That is, he considers the morphology of the head of the Zayit *bet* to be different from the 10th-century Byblian series. However, during my collations of the 10th-century Byblian Phoenician inscriptions, it became clear to me that the rounded *bet* with a large head is nicely attested in the Phoenician series. Note, for example, the forms of *bet* that are present in the ʾAḥiram Sarcophagus, with the first and third *bet* of this inscription having large heads that are as rounded as the *bet* of the Tel Zayit Abecedary. In other words, forms very similar to the Tel Zayit inscription's are found in the Byblian series of the 10th century! Note also the *bet* that is present in the Phoenician Honeyman Inscription: it is large as well. (2) Moreover, McCarter has argued that the angular form of *yod* in the Tel Zayit Abecedary is reflective of the Old Hebrew series (Tappy et al. 2006: 35). There is no doubt about the fact that the Old Hebrew *yod* is often quite angular (Rollston 1999: 76–84), but this characteristic cannot be said to be absent from the early Phoenician series. Note, for example, some of the angularity of *yod* in the ʾAḥiram Sarcophagus. Again, for the 10th century or early 9th century, angularity is not a distinctive marker (or nonmarker) of a particular script series. (3) McCarter has stated that the *qop* of the Tel Zayit inscription "is large and similar in form to the distinctive *qop* of the Gezer Calendar, with its symmetrical, two-chambered design that anticipates the subsequent history of the form. The tenth-century Phoenician prototype typically had an overall head bisected by a vertical stem, as seen in line 5 of the Yeḥimilk inscription" (Tappy et al. 2006: 39). Because McCarter refers to Yeḥimilk, I deduce that he is referring to the Phoenician forms attested at Byblos.

However, (a) note that there is no clear *qop* in the Bronze Spatula, the ʾAḥiram Sarcophagus, the ʾAbibaʿl Inscription, or the ʾElibaʿl Inscription. Thus there is a distinct dearth of data for *qop*, and I would be very reluctant to speak of a typical or prototypical form. That is, there is simply not enough data to speak of a precise Byblian Phoenician prototype. (b) Moreover, it is critical to note in this connection that the *qop* of the Yeḥimilk Inscription differs substantially from the *qop* of the Shipiṭbaʿl. Thus the two major exemplars of the 10th-century Byblian series are substantially different!

(c) Significantly, some of the forms attested in inscriptions such as the Kilamuwa and Zakkur have heads that are symmetrical and two chambered. (Note that the head of *qop* in multiple scripts was made with two semicircular strokes forming a head and a vertical stroke that often intersected the head.) (d) The cumulative evidence is quite compelling, in my opinion: I do not believe that there is anything particularly non-Phoenician about the *qop* of the Tel Zayit Abecedary.

In sum, I must differ with the proposal that the Tel Zayit Abecedary is not written in the Phoenician script. Rather, I posit that it is, in fact, written in the Phoenician script. Ultimately, (1) the suggestion that elongation is a marker of a non-Phoenician script is not, in my opinion, sustainable. Rather, elongation is something that is well attested in the 10th and 9th centuries. Of course, the fact that elongation is the norm for all three major script series (Phoenician, Aramaic, and Old Hebrew) from the 9th century through the 6th century must also be factored in as evidence demonstrating that elongation is not a feature that can be considered unique to Phoenician, Hebrew, or Aramaic. (2) Furthermore, the suggestion that certain letters of the Tel Zayit Abecedary (such as *bet*, *yod*, or *qop*) do not fit the Phoenician script series of the same horizon is problematic. Actually, these letters fit the Phoenician script series very nicely.

Naveh has argued that the first distinctive features of Hebrew writing can be discerned in the 9th century (Naveh 1987: 65). I continue to consider this position the most convincing. Though I would very much like to see evidence for the development of the Old Hebrew script in the 10th century, we do not have it. Rather, the evidence suggests that during the 10th century the ancient Israelites continued to use the prestige Phoenician script, just as did much of the rest of the Levant. Thus, based on the cumulative epigraphic evidence, I consider the Tel Zayit Abecedary to be written in a good Phoenician script of the late 10th or very early 9th century B.C.E.

Bibliography

Abou-Assaf, A.; Bordreuil, P.; and Millard, A. R.

1982 *La Statue de Tell Fekherye: Son inscription bilingue assyro-araméenne.* Études Assyriologiques. Paris: Éditions Recherche sur les civilisations.

Aharoni, Y.

1981 *Arad Inscriptions.* Jerusalem: Israel Exploration Society.

Albright, W. F.

1943 The Gezer Calendar. *BASOR* 92: 16–26.

1960 Discussion. Pp. 94–123 in *City Invincible: A Symposium on Urbanization and Cultural Development in the Ancient Near East,* ed. C. H. Kraeling and Robert M. Adams. Chicago: University of Chicago Press.

Alexandre, Y.
2006 A Canaanite-Early Phoenician Inscribed Bronze Bowl in an Iron Age IIA–B Burial Cave at Kefar Veradim, Northern Israel. *Maarav* 13: 7–41.

Aufrecht, W. E.
1989 *A Corpus of Ammonite Inscriptions*. Ancient Near Eastern Texts and Studies 4. Lewiston, NY: Edwin Mellen.

Beech, J. R.
2005 Ehri's Model of Phases of Learning to Read: A Brief Critique. *Journal of Research in Reading* 28: 50–59.

Berent, I., and Frost, R.
1997 The Inhibition of Polygraphic Consonants in Spelling Hebrew: Evidence for Recurrent Assembly of Spelling and Phonology in Visual Word Recognition. Pp. 195–219 in *Learning to Spell: Research, Theory, and Practice across Languages*, ed. C. A. Perfetti, L. Rieben, and M. Fayol. Mahway, NJ: Erlbaum.

Bosman, A. M. T., and van Orden, G. C.
1997 Why Spelling Is More Difficult Than Reading. Pp. 173–94 in *Learning to Spell: Research, Theory, and Practice across Languages*, ed. C. A. Perfetti, L. Rieben, and M. Fayol. Mahway, NJ: Erlbaum.

Brunner, H.
1991 *Altägyptische Erziehung*. Wiesbaden: Harrassowitz.

Bunimovitz, S., and Lederman, Z.
1997 Culture Conflict on Judah's Frontier. *BAR* 23/1: 42–49, 75–77.

Byrne, B.
2005 Theories of Learning to Read. Pp. 104–19 in *The Science of Reading: A Handbook*, ed. M. J. Snowling and C. Hulme. Oxford: Blackwell.

Byrne, R.
2007 The Refuge of Scribalism in Iron I Palestine. *BASOR* 345: 1–31.

Carr, D. M.
2005 *Writing on the Tablet of the Heart: Origins of Scripture and Literature*. Oxford: Oxford University Press.

Crenshaw, J. L.
1985 Education in Ancient Israel. *JBL* 104: 601–15.
1998 *Education in Ancient Israel: Across the Deadening Silence*. New York: Doubleday.

Cross, F. M.
1961 Epigraphic Notes on Hebrew Documents of the Eighth–Sixth Centuries B.C.: I. A New Reading of a Place Name in the Samaria Ostraca. *BASOR* 163: 12–14. [Repr. Cross 2003: 114–15]
1962a Epigraphic Notes on Hebrew Documents of the Eighth–Sixth Centuries B.C.: II. The Murabbaʿat Papyrus and the Letter Found near Yabneh-Yam. *BASOR* 165: 34–46. [Repr. Cross 2003: 116–24]
1962b Epigraphic Notes on Hebrew Documents of the Eighth–Sixth Centuries B.C.: III. The Inscribed Jar Handles from Gibeon. *BASOR* 168: 18–23. [Repr. Cross 2003: 125–28]

1980 Newly-Discovered Inscriptions in Old Canaanite and Early Phoenician Scripts. *BASOR* 238: 1–20. [Repr. Cross 2003: 213–30]

1995 Palaeography and the Date of the Tell Faḫariyeh Bilingual Inscription. Pp. 393–409 in *Solving Riddles and Untying Knots: Biblical, Epigraphic, and Semitic Studies in Honor of Jonas C. Greenfield*, ed. Z. Zevit, S. Gitin, and M. Sokoloff. Winona Lake, IN: Eisenbrauns. [Repr. Cross 2003: 51–60]

2003 *Leaves from an Epigrapher's Notebook: Collected Papers in Hebrew and West Semitic Palaeography and Epigraphy.* HSS 51. Winona Lake, IN: Eisenbrauns.

Cross, F. M., and Freedman, D. N.

1952 *Early Hebrew Orthography: A Study of the Epigraphic Evidence.* AOS 36. New Haven, CT: American Oriental Society.

1975 *Studies in Ancient Yahwistic Poetry.* SBLDS 21. Missoula, MT: Society of Biblical Literature.

Darnell, J. C.

2005 *Part II* of *Part I: Results of the 2001 Kerak Plateau Early Bronze Age Survey; Part II: Two Early Alphabetic Inscriptions from the Wadi el-Ḫôl*, ed. M. Chesson and J. C. Darnell et al. AASOR 59. Boston: American Schools of Oriental Research.

Degen, R.

1969 *Altaramäische Grammatik der Inschriften des 10–8 Jh v. Chr.* Wiesbaden: Harrassowitz.

Donner, H., and Röllig, W.

1979 *Kanaanäische und aramäische Inschriften.* 3 vols. 4th ed. Wiesbaden: Harrassowitz.

Ehri, L.

1997 Learning to Read and Learning to Spell Are One and the Same, Almost. Pp. 237–69 in *Learning to Spell: Research, Theory, and Practice across Languages*, ed. C. A. Perfetti, L. Rieben, and M. Fayol. Mahwah, NJ: Erlbaum.

1998 Grapheme-Phoneme Knowledge is Essential for Learning to Read Words in English. Pp. 3–40 in *Word Recognition in Beginning Literacy*, ed. J. L. Metsala and L. C. Ehri. Mahwah, NJ: Erlbaum.

2002 Phases of Acquisition in Learning to Read Words and Implications for Teaching. *British Journal of Educational Psychology: Monograph Series* 1: 7–28.

Friedrich, J., and Röllig, W.

1999 *Phönizisch-punische Grammatik.* 3rd ed. Rome: Pontifical Biblical Institute.

Frost, R.

2005 Orthographic Systems and Skilled Word Recognition Process in Reading. Pp. 272–95 in *The Science of Reading: A Handbook*, ed. M. J. Snowling and C. Hulme. Oxford: Blackwell.

Gal, Z.

1990 Khirbet Roš Zayit – Biblical Cabul: A Historical-Geographical Case. *BA* 53: 88–97.

Garr, R.
1985 *Dialect Geography of Syria-Palestine, 1000–586 B.C.E.* Philadelphia: University of Pennsylvania Press. [Repr. Winona Lake, IN: Eisenbrauns, 2004.]
George, A.
2005 In Search of the é.dub.ba.a: The Ancient Mesopotamian School in Literature and Reality. Pp. 127–37 in *An Experienced Scribe Who Neglects Nothing: Ancient Near Eastern Studies in Honor of Jacob Klein,* ed. Y. Sefati et al. Bethesda, MD: CDL.
Geva, E.
1995 Orthographic and Cognitive Processing in Learning to Read English and Hebrew. Pp. 277–91 in *Scripts and Literacy: Reading and Learning to Read Alphabets, Syllabaries and Characters,* ed. I. Taylor and D. R. Olson. Boston: Kluwer.
Gogel, S. L.
1998 *A Grammar of Epigraphic Hebrew.* SBLRBS 23. Atlanta: Scholars Press.
Gough, P. B.; Juel, C.; and Griffith, P. L.
1992 Reading, Spelling and the Orthographic Cipher. Pp. 35–48 in *Reading Acquisition,* ed. P. B. Gough, L. C. Ehri, and R. Treiman. Hillsdale, NJ: Erlbaum.
Guilleman, A. M.
1937 Le public et la vie littéraire à Rome. *Revue des Études Latines* 15: 102–21.
Haran, M.
1988 On the Diffusion of Literacy and Schools in Ancient Israel. Pp. 81–95 in *Congress Volume: Jerusalem 1986,* ed. J. A. Emerton. VTSup 40. Leiden: Brill.
Harris, W. V.
1989 *Ancient Literacy.* Cambridge: Harvard University Press.
Harris, Z. S.
1939 *Development of the Canaanite Dialects: An Investigation in Linguistic History.* AOS 16. New Haven, CT: American Oriental Society.
Havelock, E. A.
1982 *The Literate Revolution in Greece and Its Cultural Consequences.* Princeton: Princeton University Press.
Henderson, E.
1985 *Teaching: Spelling.* Boston: Houghton Mifflin.
Hess, R. S.
2002 Literacy in Iron Age Israel. Pp. 82–102 in *Windows into Old Testament History: Evidence, Argument, and the Crisis of 'Biblical Israel,'* ed. V. P. Long, D. W. Baker, and G. J. Wenham. Grand Rapids: Eerdmans.
2006 Writing about Writing: Abecedaries and Evidence for Literacy in Ancient Israel. *VT* 56: 342–46.
Hoftijzer, J., and Jongeling, K.
1995 *Dictionary of the North-West Semitic Inscriptions.* Leiden: Brill.
Jamieson-Drake, D. W.
1991 *Scribes and Schools in Monarchic Judah: A Socio-Archaeological Approach.* JSOTSup 109. Sheffield: Sheffield Academic Press.

Janssen, R., and Janssen, J. J.
1990 *Growing Up in Ancient Egypt.* London: Rubicon.
Joüon, P.
1993 *A Grammar of Biblical Hebrew: Parts 1–3.* Rev. and ed. T. Muraoka. SubBi 14/1. Rome: Pontifical Biblical Institute.
Kaufman, S. A.
1982 Reflections on the Assyrian-Aramaic Bilingual from Tell Fakhariyeh. *Maarav* 3: 137–75.
Kelm, G. L., and Mazar, A.
1995 *Timnah: A Biblical City in the Sorek Valley.* Winona Lake, IN: Eisenbrauns.
Koehler, L., and Baumgartner, W.
1994–2000 *The Hebrew and Aramaic Lexicon of the Old Testament.* 5 vols. Leiden: Brill.
Lee, S. Y.; Uttal, D. H.; and Chen, C.
1995 Writing Systems and Acquisition of Reading in American, Chinese, and Japanese First Graders. Pp. 247–63 in *Scripts and Literacy: Reading and Learning to Read Alphabets, Syllabaries and Characters,* ed. I. Taylor and D. R. Olson. Dordrecht: Kluwer Academic.
Lemaire, A.
1981 *Les écoles et la formation de la bible dans l'ancien israël.* OBO 39. Göttingen: Vandenhoeck & Ruprecht.
Levin, I.; Share, D. L.; and Shatil, E.
1996 A Qualitative-Quantitative Study of Preschool Writing: Its Development and Contribution to School Literacy. Pp. 271–93 in *The Science of Writing,* ed. M. Levy and S. Ransdell. Hillsdale, NJ: Erlbaum.
Macalister, R. A. S.
1908 Communication. *PEFQS* 40: 271.
Mazar, A.
2003 Three 10th–9th Century B.C.E. Inscriptions from Tēl Reḥôv. Pp. 171–84 in *Saxa Loquentur: Studien zur Archäologie Palästinas/Israels: Festschrift für Volkmar Fritz zum 65. Geburtstag,* ed. C. G. Hertog, U. Hübner, and S. Münger. Münster: Ugarit-Verlag.
McCarter, P. K., Jr.
1975 *The Antiquity of the Greek Alphabet.* HSM 9. Missoula, MT: Scholars Press.
McDowell, A. G.
1999 *Village Life in Ancient Egypt: Laundry Lists and Love Songs.* Oxford: Oxford University Press.
2000 Teachers and Students at Deir el-Medina. Pp. 217–33 in *Deir el-Medina in the Third Millennium* AD: *A Tribute to Jac J. Janssen,* ed. R. J. Demarée and A. Egberts. Leiden: Nederlands Instituut voor het Nabije Oosten.
Moran, W. L.
1992 *The Amarna Letters.* Baltimore: Johns Hopkins University Press.
Naveh, J.
1970 *The Development of the Aramaic Script.* Jerusalem: Israel Academy of Sciences and Humanities.
1987 *Early History of the Alphabet.* 2nd ed. Jerusalem: Magnes.

Niditch, S.
1996 *Oral World and Written Word.* Library of Ancient Israel. Louisville: Westminster John Knox.
O'Connor, M.
1990 The Ammonite Onomasticon: Syntactic and Morphological Considerations. Pp. 153–68 in *Studies in Near Eastern Culture and History in Memory of Ernest T. Abdel-Massih,* ed. J. A. Bellamy. Michigan Series on the Middle East 2. Ann Arbor: Center for Near Eastern and North African Studies, University of Michigan.
Olmo Lete, G. del, and Sanmartín, J.
2004 *A Dictionary of the Ugaritic Language in the Alphabetic Tradition.* 2nd ed. Leiden: Brill.
Peckham, B.
1968 *The Development of the Late Phoenician Scripts.* HSS 20. Cambridge: Harvard University Press.
Puech, E.
1988 Les écoles dans l'Israël préexilique: Données épigraphiques. Pp. 189–203 in *Congress Volume: Jerusalem 1986,* ed. J. A. Emerton. VTSup 40. Leiden: Brill.
Rainey, A.
1996 *Canaanite in the Amarna Tablets: A Linguistic Analysis of the Mixed Dialect Used by the Scribes from Canaan.* 4 vols. Leiden: Brill.
Ravid, D.
1995 *Language Change in Child and Adult Hebrew: A Psycholinguistic Perspective.* New York: Oxford University Press.
Richgels, D. J.
2002 Invented Spelling, Phonemic Awareness, and Reading and Writing Instruction. Pp. 142–55 in *Handbook of Early Literacy Research,* ed. S. B. Neuman and D. K. Dickinson. New York: Guilford.
Rollston, C. A.
1999 *The Script of Hebrew Ostraca of the Iron Age: 8th–6th Centuries B.C.E.* Ph.D. Dissertation. Johns Hopkins University.
2001 Ben Sira 38:24–39:11 and the *Egyptian Satire of the Trades*: A Reconsideration. *JBL* 120: 131–39.
2003 Non-Provenanced Epigraphs I: Pillaged Antiquities, Northwest Semitic Forgeries, and Protocols for Laboratory Tests. *Maarav* 10: 135–93.
2006 Scribal Education in Ancient Israel: The Old Hebrew Epigraphic Evidence. *BASOR* 344: 47–74.
Forthcoming a *Writing and Literacy in the World of Ancient Israel.* Leiden: Brill.
Forthcoming b Northwest Semitic Cursive Scripts of Iron II. In *An Eye for Form: Epigraphic Essays in Honor of Frank Moore Cross,* ed. J. Hackett and W. Aufrecht. Winona Lake, IN: Eisenbrauns.
Sanders, S.
2004 What Was the Alphabet For? The Rise of Written Vernaculars and the Making of Israelite National Literature. *Maarav* 11: 25–56.

Sass, B.
2005 *The Alphabet at the Turn of the Millennium: The West Semitic Alphabet ca. 1150–850 B.C.E.* Tel Aviv Occasional Publications 4. Tel Aviv: Yass Publications in Archaeology.
Schniedewind, W. M.
2004 *How the Bible Became a Book.* Cambridge: Cambridge University Press.
Segert, S.
1975 *Altaramaïsche Grammatik.* Leipzig: Verlag Enzyklopädie.
1976 *A Grammar of Phoenician and Punic.* Munich: Beck.
1984 *A Basic Grammar of the Ugaritic Language.* Berkeley: University of California Press.
Seymour, P. H. K.
1997 Foundations of Orthographic Development. Pp. 319–37 in *Learning to Spell: Research, Theory, and Practice across Languages,* ed. C. A. Perfetti, L. Rieben, and M. Fayol. Mahwah, NJ: Erlbaum.
2005 Early Reading Development in European Orthographies. Pp. 296–315 in *The Science of Reading: A Handbook,* ed. M. J. Snowling and C. Hulme. Oxford: Blackwell.
Share, D. L., and Levin, I.
1999 Learning to Read and Write in Hebrew. Pp. 89–111 in *Learning to Read and Write: A Cross-Linguistic Perspective,* ed. M. Harris and G. Hatano. Cambridge: Cambridge University Press.
Tappy, R. E.; McCarter, P. K.; Lundberg, M.; and Zuckerman, B.
2006 An Abecedary of the Mid-Tenth Century from the Judaean Shephelah. *BASOR* 344: 5–46.
Tinney, S.
1998 Texts, Tablets, and Teaching: Scribal Education at Nippur and Ur. *Expedition* 40/2: 40–50.
1999 On the Curricular Setting of Sumerian Literature. *Iraq* 61: 159–72.
Toorn, K. van der
2007 *Scribal Culture and the Making of the Hebrew Bible.* Cambridge: Harvard University Press.
Totereau, C.; Thevenin, M.; and Fayol, M.
1997 Pp. 97–114 in *Learning to Spell: Research, Theory, and Practice across Languages,* ed. C. A. Perfetti, L. Rieben, and M. Fayol. Mahwah, NJ: Erlbaum.
Treiman, R.
1993 *Beginning to Spell: A Study of First-Grade Children.* New York: Oxford University Press.
Treiman, R., and Kessler, B.
2005 Writing Systems and Spelling Development. Pp. 121–34 in *The Science of Reading: A Handbook,* ed. M. J. Snowling and C. Hulme. Oxford: Blackwell.
Tropper, J.
2000 *Ugaritische Grammatik.* AOAT 273. Münster: Ugarit-Verlag.

Vanstiphout, H. L. J.
1979 How Did They Learn Sumerian? *JCS* 31: 118–26.
Veldhuis, N.
2003 Mesopotamian Canons. Pp. 9–28 in *Homer, the Bible and Beyond: Literary and Religious Canons in the Ancient World*, ed. M. Finkelberg and G. G. Stroumsa. Leiden: Brill.
Waltke, B., and O'Connor, M.
1990 *An Introduction to Biblical Hebrew Syntax*. Winona Lake, IN: Eisenbrauns.
Weeks, S.
1994 *Early Israelite Wisdom*. Oxford: Clarendon.
Wimmer, H., and Landerl, K.
1997 How Learning to Spell German Differs from Learning to Spell English. Pp. 81–96 in *Learning to Spell: Research, Theory, and Practice across Languages*, ed. C. A. Perfetti, L. Rieben, and M. Fayol. Mahwah, NJ: Erlbaum.
Yadin, Y.; Aharoni, Y.; Amiran, R.; Dothan, T.; Dunayevsky, I.; and Perrot, J.
1960 *Hazor II: An Account of the Second Season of Excavations, 1956*. Jerusalem: Magnes.
Yadin, Y.; Aharoni, Y.; Amiran, R.; Ben-Tor, A.; Dothan, M.; Dothan, T.; Dunayevsky, I.; Geva, S.; and Stern, E.
1961 *Hazor III–IX: An Account of the Third and Fourth Seasons of Excavations, 1957–1958*. Jerusalem: Magnes.
Young, I.
1998a Israelite Literacy: Interpreting the Evidence, Part 1. *VT* 48: 239–53.
1998b Israelite Literacy: Interpreting the Evidence, Part 2. *VT* 48: 408–22.
2005 Israelite Literacy and Inscriptions: A Response to Richard Hess. *VT* 54: 565–67.
Zevit, Z.
1980 *Matres Lectionis in Ancient Hebrew Epigraphs*. ASOR Monographs 2. Cambridge, MA: American Schools of Oriental Research.

Writing and Early Iron Age Israel: Before National Scripts, Beyond Nations and States

Seth L. Sanders
Trinity College, Hartford, CT

With the newly discovered Tel Zayit Abecedary taking its place beside the well-known Gezer Calendar, we now have two extended texts from 10th-century Israel, alongside perhaps four one-word inscriptions (Tappy et al. 2006: 28). These texts represent the first writing in Canaan to diverge from Phoenician (till then the only form of alphabetic writing in the Iron Age), thus making them the earliest distinct ancestors of Hebrew. Kyle McCarter has argued that paleographically the Tel Zayit Abecedary and the Gezer Calendar stand at an intermediate point between the contemporary Phoenician and later southern Canaanite scripts by displaying features of the emerging inland script style well known from Iron IIB Israel, Judah, and Moab (Tappy et al. 2006).[1] Their paleography, at least, represents an organic development toward Hebrew and its relatives.

But if the paleography of our 10th-century inscriptions shows signs of evolution toward Hebrew (and southern Canaanite) scripts, does their content show signs of a similar evolution toward an Israelite (or southern Canaanite) state? Did they, for example, serve the purposes of a bureaucracy? By comparing the 10th-century evidence from Israel with texts from contemporary Phoenicia and later Israel, we can begin to situate this material in the history of written West Semitic culture.

One way to think about the Tel Zayit Abecedary is that it represents a snapshot that captured an Israelite state in the process of development. Just as the script forms could be interpreted as a midpoint in the evolution from Phoenician to Hebrew, so also we can perhaps catch from them a glimpse of David's confederacy of bandits and tribal leaders as they

1. For detailed counterarguments that the elongation McCarter sees as a taxonomically crucial inland feature is in fact widespread in 10th- and 9th-century Northwest Semitic inscriptions, see Rollston in this volume, pp. 61ff.

evolved into a kingdom. But what if there existed a rich, complex culture in 10th-century Israel that could produce texts but was not a state? If the debate has tended either to affirm or deny a state, how could we think about forms of communication or politics that go beyond this binarism?

In fact, all the data at our disposal suggest that, if we want to use inscriptions to think about 10th-century Israel, we must go beyond the state/nonstate paradigm. Our evidence is limited but clear in what it says. The two major inscriptions we have from Israel display patterns that are obviously different from the texts of the contemporary Phoenician and later Iron Age kingdoms.

The 10th-century Byblian Phoenician inscriptions of ʾAḥiram and his successors are the memorials of a local ruler. Claiming no territory beyond the city of Byblos, they express no broader political ambitions. Each one of the five known 10th-century monumental Phoenician texts (*KAI* 1, 4, 5, 6, 7) is a royal dedicatory inscription the main topic of which is the very object on which it is inscribed. Acting to label the object on which it is inscribed, each sentence has deictic force:[2]

KAI 1: *ʾrn.z pˁl.[ʾ]tbˁl*	(This is) the sarcophagus that ʾIttobaˁl made.
KAI 4: *bt.z bny.yḥmlk*	(This is) the temple that Yeḥimilk built.
KAI 5: [*mš z y*]*bʾ.ʾbbˁl*	([This is) the cultic image] that ʾAbibaˁl [se]t up.
KAI 6: *mš. z pˁl .ʾlbˁl*	(This is) the cultic image that ʾElibaˁl made.
KAI 7: *qr. z bny. šptbˁl*	(This is) the wall that Shipiṭbaˁl built.

This sarcophagus, this temple, this wall was made by the king: the inscriptions refer to no broader political or military actions. No territories are annexed here, no peoples made to submit to Baal and his king. Neither do these Phoenician royal inscriptions "ventriloquize" the king by speaking in his voice in the first person ("I built . . . ," as every Mesopotamian king worth his salt claimed) but, rather, refer anonymously to the object. As memorials of one-time ritual acts intended to shore up the king's rule over his home city, they do not chronicle those acts of public ambition and organized violence that make up most written history from the ancient Near East.

When we find the first extended alphabetic texts in southern Canaan, in the late 9th and 8th centuries, we suddenly encounter something like history. The Meshaʿ Stele, the Kuntillet ʿAjrud inscriptions, and the Sa-

2. The single exception is *KAI* 5, where the beginning is damaged, but a reference to the object is the only plausible reconstruction, given the rigidly stereotyped genre and the pervasive parallels. For the sake of simplicity the transcriptions follow the readings of *KAI*, and the translations leave off the titles and relationships following the donor's name in each original inscription.

maria Ostraca display the various voices and registers of state religion, royal bureaucracy, and professional scribal training. The Meshaʿ Stele is the first text in the south to speak in the first-person voice of the king: not "*This* is the stele Meshaʿ set up" but "*I am* Meshaʿ, son of Kemoshyat, king of Moab." This inscription "ventriloquizes" Meshaʿ, as though the king is standing before us and addressing us.

The Meshaʿ inscription's use of the royal first person is an unrecognized landmark in West Semitic literature. As part of a wave of West-Semitic first-person royal inscriptions that appear across the Levant (including the Tel Dan and Zakkur inscriptions) in the late 9th century, it is without precedent in the history of alphabetic writing. Despite their wealth, cosmopolitanism, and facility with writing (shown in no fewer than eight languages and five scripts at Ugarit!), Meshaʿ's West-Semitic-speaking Late Bronze Age ancestors never produced anything of the sort.[3] Neither Ugarit nor Emar showed any interest in public royal monuments or historical accounts chronicling the mighty deeds of king or state. Mesopotamian culture had been widely distributed for well over a thousand years, and inscriptions of the type "I am Hammurapi, king of Babylon, great king, king of kings" were famous. Yet the alphabetic writers who had full access to Mesopotamian high culture chose to avoid this genre in their own writing. Prior to this point, there is no tradition of first-person royal alphabetic inscriptions.

It is in the Kuntillet ʿAjrud inscriptions, probably from the beginning of the 8th century B.C.E., that we find the first trappings of statehood in Hebrew writing. Among the varying alphabets splashed across Pithos Two, we recognize a practice letter "to my lord" from a military or bureaucratic subordinate to a superior. On the wall, we find a hymn praising El and Baal as military gods, who make the mountains shudder on the day of battle. The Samaria Ostraca represent the first evidence in Canaan of alphabetic record keeping for the purposes of taxation or tribute. It is in the 9th and 8th centuries that we first begin to see in the linear alphabet what Ryan Byrne (forthcoming) has cuttingly termed "the cosmetics of statecraft" – the highly specialized items that advertise the presence of a territorial political power: "the state was here."

3. The crucial point about a lack of Late-Bronze-Age West-Semitic interest in chronicles comes from Mark S. Smith (2007). A comprehensive argument for this point is made in Sanders (forthcoming: chap. 4). The eight written languages of Ugarit were Sumerian, Akkadian, Hittite, Luwian, Hurrian, Ugaritic, Egyptian, and Cypro-Minoan. The five scripts were syllabic cuneiform, alphabetic cuneiform, Luwian Hieroglyphic, Egyptian Hieroglyphic, and Cypro-Minoan. See, conveniently, Bordreuil and Pardee 2004: 1.20.

If the 10th-century Phoenician inscriptions are memorials of a local dynasty and the 9th-century Moabite and 8th-century Hebrew texts are monumental or bureaucratic messages from a state, the Gezer Calendar and the Tel Zayit Abecedary together stand a world apart. For these inscriptions comprise lists that delineate the correct order of things that are used – the months of the year and the letters of the alphabet – to order a world. In other words, they look like items used in training bureaucrats. But here is where the orders represented in the Gezer and Zayit inscriptions part ways with both Phoenician and Israelite state culture.

Bureaucracies in the ancient Near East are intimately connected with the coercive tools of statecraft: taxation and standing armies.[4] The bureaucracy makes systematic taxation possible by keeping track of who owes what and when. Bureaucratic tax collection in turn creates the concentration of wealth needed to support the army, whose soldiers the bureaucrats keep paid and fed on a regular basis (and who in turn can threaten or kill people who do not pay their taxes). An absolutely essential feature, which in fact we find in every Mesopotamian city-state from the invention of writing on, is the regimentation of time: breaking the year down into discrete, even units. The months may be numbered or they may be named – after local festivals, for example – but they must be uniform: twelve uniform months per year.[5] As 1 Kgs 4:7 says of Solomon, "And Solomon had twelve officers over all Israel, which provided victuals for the king and his household: each man his month in a year made provision."

The Gezer Calendar, by contrast with the Israelite and Phoenician calendars, and unlike every state calendar known in the entire history of ancient Near Eastern bureaucracy, does not break up time into even, quantifiable units:

A couple of months (*yarḥêw*, in the dual) of gathering
A couple of months of early sowing
A couple of months of late sowing
A month of making hay
A month of harvesting barley
A month of harvest and finishing
A couple of months of vine pruning
A month of summer fruit.[6]

4. A provocative and thoughtful recent exploration of the relationship between bureaucracy and violence is Graeber 2006.

5. A comprehensive study of local Mesopotamian calendars is available in Cohen 1983.

6. My translation largely follows Pardee 1997.

The Gezer Calendar encompasses eight months in an uneven order: three double months, then three single months, then a double month, then a single month. Following the flow of human labor tied to the ecology of northern Israel, it is more a calendar of seasons than of months. Thus it does not give numbers or proper names to these months. Rather than being ordered by human political designations – name, as in the Phoenician or postexilic Judean systems (*yeraḥ hāʾētānîm*; *ḥōdeš ʾĕlûl*), or number, as in the Israelite and Judean systems (for example, month two) – it is ordered by the passage of agricultural seasons.

These loose, colloquial months cannot plausibly be the months of the biblical lunisolar calendar, with its humanly imposed and symmetrical 30-day units and intercalary months. The lack of fit between the actual 365+-day year and the postulated 360 days of the lunisolar ritual calendar requires systematic bureaucratic adjustment; otherwise, after a few decades of twelve 30-day months, the "month of summer fruit" would come solidly in the middle of winter. This inevitability is not a difficulty for the Gezer Calendar, which lists environmentally based seasons ("harvesting" can only come after the actual weather has permitted things to grow), not bureaucratically designated time units.

The Gezer Calendar is primary evidence of a phenomenon as culturally significant as bureaucratic training – the "literization," the setting down in writing – of local culture.[7] Although the organization of the Gezer Calendar is useless for teaching bureaucrats, its language connects to an old, pan-Canaanite vocabulary of timekeeping. The Gezer Calendar uses the common Canaanite term for month: *yarḥ*, which we find in Phoenician inscriptions. The only instances in which it appears in the Hebrew Bible with the name of a month are in three citations from the annals of Solomon as reported by the book of Kings (1 Kgs 6:37, 38; 8:2). We learn the standard dating system of the Israelite monarchy from the glosses by which Kings translates the old Canaanite dating system: *bĕyeraḥ bûl hûʾ haḥōdeš haššĕmînî* 'the moon of Bul [it is month VIII in our dating system]' (1 Kgs 6:38). The standard and uniform format of Kings' dating fits that of the Arad Ostraca, which does not name months but numbers them.[8]

The very need to translate the old Canaanite months into "Israelite Standard Time" suggests that the calendar system of Solomon is not the innovation of a new bureaucracy but a relic borrowed from the then-dominant written culture: the Phoenician of Canaanite scribes. The most

7. For the idea and its consequences in a Near Eastern context, see Pollock 2006.

8. An excellent treatment of the different dating systems in use in the Iron Age Levant is Lemaire 1998.

plausible explanation of this evidence is that people were indeed writing annals for Solomon, but these people were not yet aware of the calendar of the Israelite state.

The Tel Zayit Abecedary, similarly, has two alphabet letter-orders found in no Israelite abecedary (assuming with McCarter that the *l-k* order is a mistake), one of which is known only from the earlier Canaanite alphabetic order found at ʿIzbet Ṣarṭah.

Iron Age Hebrew

Consonants	*ʾ b g d h w ḥ ḫ z ṭ y k l m n s p ʿ ǵ ṣ q r ś š t*
ʿIzbet Ṣarṭah	*ʾ b g d h w ḥ z ṭ y k l m n s p ʿ ṣ q r š t*
Tel Zayit	*ʾ b g d w h ḥ z ṭ y l ˣ k m n s p ʿ ṣ q r š t*
Majority IA IIB	*ʾ b g d h w z ḥ ṭ y k l m n s p ʿ ṣ q r š t*
Minority IA IIB	*ʾ b g d h w z ḥ ṭ y k l m n s ʿ p ṣ q r š t*

The Tel Zayit Abecedary has more features in common with pre-Israelite alphabetic orders than with known Israelite and Judean orders. Note in the chart above that, of the three "reversals" from the late order we consider standard, two appear to exist in the 12th-century ʿIzbet Ṣarṭah abecedary, while only one, the *pe-ʿayin* order, is known to have survived past the 10th century. Furthermore, the *pe-ʿayin* order may well have been the most popular Iron Age alphabetic order: Christopher Rollston has demonstrated that Iron Age Hebrew scribes had a distinctive and completely consistent way of writing *samek* and *pe* in sequence. From this discovery, Ryan Byrne has drawn the logical conclusion that this graphic sequence resulted from training in an alphabetical order in which *pe* directly followed *samek*.[9] But this sequence is unknown in the standard Ugaritic abecedaries that represent the first evidence of the *ʾ-b-g-d* order. Indeed, it may well have arisen through influence from a completely different alphabetic tradition that was known at Ugarit and in Israel, the southern *halḥam* order, which arranges the letters *samek-ʾalep-pe-ʿayin.*[10] The presence of the *samek* before *pe* and *ʿayin* could well have triggered the reversal – the ghostly trace of a different order entirely.

9. Rollston (2003: 160–62) showed that in all Iron Age Hebrew inscriptions in which *samek* and *pe* are adjacent, the *samek* rises to an unusual height and the *pe* is placed unusually low on the line. Byrne (2007: 4–5) then argued that this sequence is an artifact of scribal training in an abecedary in which *pe* came before *ʿayin*.

10. On this order, see my edition of the Beth-shemesh abecedary in Horowitz, Oshima, and Sanders 2006: 157–60, with bibliography.

The two, extended, 10th-century linear alphabetic texts currently available to us from Israel cannot plausibly have been the tools of state bureaucracy. The paucity of evidence, however, requires that we remain open to various explanations until more data emerge to solidify the picture. While the texts' content definitely does not fit a "curriculum," it is possible that they were secondarily related to a curriculum: the Zayit Abecedary could be the work of a particularly bad writer, the reversals being his first attempts at engraving a more standard alphabet. The Gezer Calendar could represent an experiment with "literizing," an attempt to put a folk song or almanac into writing. Indeed elsewhere – in early modern France, for example – almanacs of folk wisdom were put in writing not by peasant farmers but precisely when intellectuals became interested in recording and distributing the ideas of the "folk" (see Davis 1978).

What remains true is that we do not have a shred of evidence for a state curriculum in the 10th century. This absence could be an accident of preservation, but it fits a pattern that is becoming well attested with the new archaeological discoveries in the City of David and Tel Reḥov. One of the most striking features of Hebrew writing, when we have it in full force in Israel and Judah during the 8th through 6th centuries, is its presence on seals. There are approximately 90 provenanced seals, impressions, and bullas from the Iron Age recorded in Avigad and Sass's invaluable (though unwieldy) collection of inscribed West Semitic seals.[11] What is so important about the seals and bullas is that a significant range of people, from officials to untitled individuals, seem to be using writing in this period as a kind of emblem. As Millard notes (1999), the proportion of inscriptions on these artifacts is far higher than on Assyrian and Babylonian seals from the period. But not one is archaeologically dated before the 8th century.

As we find more and more seals from earlier periods in Israel, it is becoming clear that scribes and bureaucrats in these periods, at least in Judah, were not as interested in writing as officials were in later centuries. Excavations at Tel Reḥov and the City of David have now yielded a mass of around 190 well-stratified seals and seal impressions from the 10th and 9th centuries.[12] Yet in contrast to the abundant Hebrew seals of the 8th to 6th centuries, not a single excavated seal from the 10th- or 9th-century Levant

11. For many of these seals, even when the excavation report gives a date for its context, Avigad and Sass (1997) do not report that date.

12. See briefly the statement of Mazar 2007 and in more detail the recent publication of Reich, Shukron, and Lernau 2007. While the seal impressions from late-9th-century Jerusalem appear on bullas (clay pieces used to close papyrus documents), we do not know whether the documents were written in Phoenician, Hebrew, or another language.

is inscribed with its owner's name. Going by the current evidence, then, royal officials before the 8th century were not interested in their names' being represented on seals.

What is so provocative about the epigraphic data is that they challenge both the somewhat idealized reconstruction of a bureaucratized Solomonic state and the somewhat preconceived dismissal of complex culture in 10th-century Israel. Thus the two major 10th-century inscriptions that we have seem to represent a craft tradition that had not yet been domesticated, tied to a state bureaucracy. Although neither the Tel Zayit Abecedary nor the Gezer Calendar bears marks of a state, both suggest another way to think about how Israel may have become a state and how it came to be remembered as a state.

Let us go back to the early history of alphabetic writing to place our data in their framework. First, it is worth remembering that much of the earliest alphabetic writing has not yet been deciphered. Gordon Hamilton's careful treatment (2006) of the first known alphabetic texts from Egypt shows that a large amount of what is written in Proto-Sinaitic is incomprehensible by current modes of reading. There seem to be three main possibilities, all of which exclude any standardizing influence by West-Semitic bureaucracies or scribes. First, the language being written could be mostly non-Semitic, with West-Semitic phrases such as "beloved of the Lady" mixed in.[13] Second, the correspondences between the letters and sounds could be significantly different from their correspondences in the Late Bronze and Iron Ages. Finally, they could follow *genre conventions* that are not known in later West-Semitic texts. Influenced by local Egyptian inscriptions, they could be communicating information that we have not been prepared to read, as Kyle McCarter argues in a forthcoming study. We have the same difficulty with the longest linear alphabetic text from Late Bronze Age Israel, the ʿIzbet Ṣarṭah Ostracon, though due to the poor quality of the inscription's execution we should not rule out its being mere gibberish. And outside ʿIzbet Ṣarṭah there is no evidence of anything "curricular" in the linear alphabet before the Iron Age IIB period.

In fact, this lack of an extensive early alphabetic curriculum also fits the pattern of Ugarit, where there is very little clear evidence of didactic texts in Ugaritic beyond the abecedaries. The scribes of Ugarit learned to write

13. The phrase *mʾhb bʿlt* 'beloved of the Lady', spelled three different ways (!), appears in a minimum of three Proto-Sinaitic inscriptions, a reading confirmed by a parallel Egyptian inscription, *mry ḥtḥr* [*nbt*] *mfkt* 'Beloved of Hathor [lady of] turquoise' (see Hamilton 2006: 332–35). Hamilton reads the phrase in Sinai 345, 353, and 374 (see 2006: 334, 348, 372), while Sass considers the reading possible in up to eight inscriptions (adding 348, 350, 351, 354, and 356; see Sass 1988: 12–27).

mainly by means of training in the Mesopotamian cuneiform tradition. The solution here probably lies in what the Ugaritologist Robert Hawley (2008) points out about scribal training: unlike when individuals were writing in Sumerian and Akkadian, for whom learning a writing system necessarily also entailed learning two interlaced alien languages, "Ugaritic scribes did not need to be taught their own language." The reason there was so little scribal training in West Semitic before the late Iron Age is that writing was understood as linguistically transparent. Technically, learning it was thought not to require much curriculum beyond the alphabet itself.

All these examples show that there is more than one possible fit between writing and political development — the history of the ancient Near East attests multiple relationships between scripts and states. Unlike in Mesopotamia, the West-Semitic evidence suggests that the linear alphabet lived for a thousand years or more, from its invention around 2000 B.C.E. to the 9th century, without a state patron. Even the early Phoenician royal inscriptions of the 10th century do not make political claims; they are evidence more likely of highly skilled craftsmen than of bureaucrats.

How can we conceptualize the independence of the linear alphabet from the state until a relatively late period? Here we should remind ourselves of some basic facts about the relationship between writing and political organization. First, writing does not necessitate the existence of a state; in fact, even the production of massive amounts of writing does not necessitate the existence of a state. The Old Assyrian caravan archive has produced tens of thousands of texts sent by merchants; the texts refer to scribes not of the palace or temple but the *kārum*, the merchant colony. Moving slightly later, it is a well-known fact in Indology that Sanskrit was spread across south Asia (ignoring numerous political boundaries) by Buddhist monasteries, not kings (see Kelly 2006). And in the modern period, "nongovernmental organizations" such as Islamic schools generated (mostly male) literacy in villages without plumbing, as Ivor Wilks's remarkable study of Islamic writing in southern Sudan already pointed out in 1968.

In fact, social complexity can happen with or without a state: if a state is not needed to organize extensive literary production, as Buddhism and Islam widely attest, neither is a state needed to organize large-scale economic or military activities. In the ancient Near East, the best-known and most effective nonstate organizers of violence were various social groups, named "Amorite" and "Aramean" by the states they alternately threatened, conquered, and helped to create.[14] As Fleming (2004) has recently

14. For a thoughtful and up-to-date treatment, see Younger 2007a.

shown, the leaders who famously conquered the Old Babylonian city-state of Mari on the upper Euphrates during the time of Hammurapi thought about themselves and organized their activities along largely tribal lines. In an earlier period, during the Early Bronze Age, nomadic groups organized large-scale copper-smelting "factories" in the Faynan area of Jordan. Russell Adams's work (2006) demonstrates that the seasonally and regionally organized metal-forging and distribution systems operated with no significant contribution from the nearby city-states. Finally, regarding a later period, Raz Kletter's detailed study (1998) of the Judean system of weights argues that detailed and consistent standards for counting units of trade were created by a network of merchants. Even during the days of the Kingdom of Judah, royal shekels were few and far between.

The simplest explanation for the persistence of the linear alphabet between the Late Bronze Age collapse and the Iron IIB renaissance of writing is that writing was a small-scale luxury craft (Byrne 2007). The goal of these scribes' work was to signify local powers such as the king of Amurru (witness the arrowheads bearing his name) but through inscriptions on portable luxury items such as engraved weapons, not monuments. The linear alphabet's durability was tied to a small-scale, adaptable craft tradition serving elites but free of allegiance to any specific dialect or regime.[15]

Intriguingly, the one exception to Byrne's pattern may be the survival not of cuneiform but of hieratic. It has been pointed out that the specific forms of the hieratic numerals seem to have their ancestry not in the Iron Age but in the Late Bronze Age.[16] During the Late Bronze Age/Iron Age transition, bookkeeping also may have been the province not of state bureaucrats but of private craftsmen and entrepreneurs.

Israelite writing, then, would appear with the emergence of a curriculum perhaps at the end of the 9th century. Kuntillet ʿAjrud provides a constellation of material suggesting that a standard written Hebrew had been configured as a state tool. Together for the first time we see practice texts:

---

15. Perhaps "elite" is an inadequate term here. We tend to give explanations from the viewpoint of patron or consumer, but what if we think of writing from the viewpoint of its producers? Doing so might entail seeing them as entrepreneurs of knowledge who held a monopoly on a specialized craft. Certainly in Greece, where the early alphabet spread quite independently of schools (the main topics of the earliest Greek writing being drinking, dancing, sex, and the ownership of objects), this monopoly can be explicitly defended when it comes to writing. Greek laws at Crete included provision for the "exclusive right" to write in a town (Gagarin 2003: 66–67).

16. See Lemaire and Vernus 1983; Goldwasser 1991. For a countervailing view, expressed in general terms, see Wimmer 2006.

abecedaries with two variant alphabetic orders, hymns to national war-gods, and practice letters that not only reflected but also enshrined social hierarchy by addressing the receiver as *ʾădōnî* 'my lord'.

The emergence of an alphabetic curriculum in the southern Levant is tied to the emergence of history-writing itself. As Mark Smith has recently (2007) pointed out, history was not a native West-Semitic genre. In the Late Bronze Age, at neither Ugarit nor Emar do we find annals of events; even 500 years earlier, the only chronicle from the West-Semitic-dominated city-state of Mari was from Šamši-Adad, which followed (or perhaps, inaugurated?) Assyrian conventions of genre. Instead what we find are indications, scattered through ritual and political procedures, that the people, not just the king, were considered agents of history and religion (see briefly Sanders 2004 and, more extensively, Sanders forthcoming).

Nadav Naʾaman has suggested the pathway by which written history came to the Levant: in the early 9th century, we first hear of Neo-Assyrian kings such as Shalmaneser III placing monuments with inscriptions in the royal voice at borders and boundaries between Syria, Phoenicia, and Israel (Naʾaman 2006).[17] A generation later, we see the first signs of local kings and kingdoms using writing in their own scripts. For the first time, public alphabetic inscriptions speak in the voice of local kings. They tell stories about the life of the state – the buildings the king has built and the people he has killed.

The view required by the evidence, then, is not that an Israelite state established writing but that writing was recruited by an Israelite state to establish itself, in order to argue publicly that it existed. If hieratic (and perhaps alphabetic) scribalism is what *survived* the Late Bronze Age/Iron Age transition, it was not what was being created by a state in this period but what the state was coopting for its own purposes. We do not need to search for an Israelite state as the source of a complex Iron Age culture but the other way around. As Bruce Routledge's study of Moabite writing and politics (2000) suggests, the Moabite kingdom did not simply evolve out of tribes; rather, King Meshaʿ used writing to persuade people with a tribal ideology to think of themselves differently, to see themselves as part of his kingdom. The kingdom of Moab was in a crucial way a redescription of what was already there: a new way to represent local communities, not just to kill people and take their possessions. The state was at least as much a way of communicating as it was a way of coercing or redistributing.

But exactly to whom are these inscriptions written? Over the past half-century of social theory, interest in the interplay between communicative

17. For a detailed study of the most influential 9th-century Neo-Assyrian king's relations with the Levant, see Younger 2007b.

and political forms has blossomed. One phenomenon that the most intellectually interesting and historically grounded social theorists have discovered repeatedly is what Jürgen Habermas and Michael Warner called a public – a political community called into being through the circulation of texts. Texts that address people in a vernacular – a written version of their own spoken language – can help call this people into existence as a self-conscious group. Habermas, Warner, and, most famously, Benedict Anderson recognized this process at work in the beginnings of the modern era (Habermas 1989 [orig. 1962]; Warner 2002; Anderson 1991).[18] Perhaps unsurprisingly, each observed it in the materials he had been studying and attributed it to the period in which he encountered it. Habermas called it "the public sphere," Warner simply "a public," and Anderson "the nation." Each assumed that it was a side effect of the uniquely modern processes with which he was familiar.

Fascinatingly, something like a public may have emerged already in the Iron Age Levant, far from modern ideologies of the nation-state and in a drastically different communicative situation. Instead of the capitalist idea of books and newspapers circulating as commodities that everybody might want to buy, there existed then the idea of written texts circulating through the process of *QR*ʾ 'summoning/reading/proclaiming', represented repeatedly in the Bible and West-Semitic inscriptions as an inherently public and political act.[19] If this hypothesis is accurate, then we stand to gain the most, not by recognizing how this ideology resembled nationalism, but by learning how it was different – how did people in the Levant rethink forms of communication to create their own kinds of participation? Historically, where did these notions of participation come from, and what happened to them with the invention of written Hebrew?

What we may be catching in the act with the 10th-century Israelite inscriptions is the slowly increasing definition and sophistication of a form of writing that had long lived outside the chancery. The possibility of

18. For an earlier statement on the possibilities that Anderson's work could suggest for biblical studies, see Sanders 2004. For an alternative history of the relations between communicative and political form in premodern South Asia, see Pollock 2007. Pollock's astoundingly richly-documented study uses new theoretical constructs that flow from the material he considers and is not dependent on the concepts of either *public* or *nation*.

19. For a brilliant exposition of the biblical ideology of reading, see Boyarin 1993, and compare the double publication, visual and aural, of the 8th-century Aramaic Sefire vassal treaty, in which the parties are commanded, "Let not one word of this text be silent," and which concludes, "thus we have said and thus we have written" (Sefire I A 13, B 8–9, C 1–3).

history-writing in the Levant emerged as local kings learned from Mesopotamian empires how to make old craft traditions of linear alphabetic writing speak for the first time in the voice of a state. This royal history was, in turn, borrowed and rethought by writers responsible to communities outside the royal court to create a different form of history in ancient Israel. In my forthcoming *Invention of Hebrew*, I have argued in detail that what is distinctive about the written Hebrew version of history is that it places the people, alongside the king, as a protagonist of events – an idea that can be traced to a long and well-attested line of West-Semitic, tribal political thought. The rethinking of cosmopolitan imperial language in terms of local culture was a groundbreaking event that produced West-Semitic vernacular writing. The Bible's history then became possible when a group of people began to be addressed through texts as a public. The Zayit and Gezer inscriptions suggest that alphabetic writing is being deliberately adapted to local forms outside a scribal center. If so, they are the first signs in the Iron Age of a new possibility: biblical history.

Bibliography

Adams, Russell B.

2006 Copper Trading Networks across the Wadi Arabah during the Later Early Bronze Age. Pp. 137–44 in *Crossing the Rift: Resources, Routes, Settlement Patterns and Interaction in the Wadi Arabah*, ed. P. Bienkowski and K. Galor. London: Council for British Research in the Levant.

Anderson, Benedict

1991 *Imagined Communities: Reflections on the Origin and Spread of Nationalism.* Rev. ed. London: Verso. [original, 1983]

Avigad, Nahman, and Sass, Benjamin

1997 *Corpus of West Semitic Stamp Seals.* Jerusalem: Israel Academy of Sciences and Humanities / Israel Exploration Society.

Bordreuil, Pierre, and Pardee, Dennis

2004 *Manuel d'ougaritique.* 2 vols. Paris: Geuthner.

Boyarin, Daniel

1993 Placing Reading: Ancient Israel and Medieval Europe. Pp. 10–37 in *The Ethnography of Reading*, ed. J. Boyarin. Berkeley: University of California Press.

Byrne, Ryan

2007 The Refuge of Scribalism in Iron I Palestine. *BASOR* 345: 1–31.

forthcoming *Statecraft in Ancient Israel: An Archaeology of the Political Sciences.* Winona Lake, IN: Eisenbrauns.

Cohen, Mark E.

1993 *The Cultic Calendars of the Ancient Near East.* Bethesda, MD: CDL.

Davis, Natalie Zemon
1975 Proverbial Wisdom and Popular Errors. Pp. 227–67 in *Society and Culture in Early Modern France.* Stanford, CA: Stanford University Press.
Donner, H., and Röllig, W.
1962–64 *Kanaanäische und aramäische Inschriften.* 3 vols. Wiesbaden: Harrassowitz.
Fleming, Daniel
2004 *Democracy's Ancient Ancestors: Mari and Early Collective Governance.* Cambridge: Cambridge University Press.
Gagarin, Michael
2003 Letters of the Law: Written Texts in Archaic Greek Law. Pp. 59–77 in *Written Texts and the Rise of Literate Culture in Ancient Greece,* ed. H. Yunis. Cambridge: Cambridge University Press.
Goldwasser, O.
1991 An Egyptian Scribe from Lachish and the Hieratic Tradition of the Hebrew Kingdoms. *TA* 18: 248–53.
Graeber, David
2006 Beyond Power/Knowledge: An Exploration of the Relation of Power, Ignorance, and Stupidity. Malinowski Memorial Lecture, London School of Economics, May 25, 2006. Available at: *http://www.lse.ac.uk/collections/LSEPublicLecturesAndEvents/pdf/20060525-Graeber.pdf.*
Habermas, Jürgen
1989 *The Structural Transformation of the Public Sphere: An Inquiry into a Category of Bourgeois Society,* trans. T. Burger with the assistance of F. Lawrence. Cambridge, MA: MIT Press.
Hamilton, Gordon J.
2006 *The Origins of the West Semitic Alphabet in Egyptian Scripts.* CBQMS 40. Washington, DC: Catholic Biblical Association.
Haran, Menachem
1988 On the Diffusion of Literacy and Schools in Ancient Israel. Pp. 81–95 in *Congress Volume: Jerusalem, 1986,* ed. J. A. Emerton. VTSup 40. Leiden: Brill.
Hawley, Robert
2008 On the Alphabetic Scribal Curriculum at Ugarit. Pp. 57–67 in *Proceedings of the 51st Rencontre Assyriologique Internationale, Held at the Oriental Institute of the University of Chicago, July 18–22, 2005,* ed. Robert D. Biggs, Jennie Myers, and Martha T. Roth. SAOC 62. Chicago: Oriental Institute.
Horowitz, Wayne; Oshima, Takayoshi; and Sanders, Seth L.
2006 *Cuneiform in Canaan and the Land of Israel: Cuneiform Sources from the Land of Israel in Ancient Times.* Jerusalem: Israel Exploration Society and Hebrew University.
KAI = Donner and Röllig 1962–64
Kelly, John
2006 Writing and the State: India, China and General Definitions. Pp. 15–32 in *Margins of Writing, Origins of Cultures: New Approaches to Writing and Reading in the Ancient Near East,* ed. S. Sanders. Chicago: Oriental Institute.

Kletter, Raz

1998 *Economic Keystones: The Weight System of the Kingdom of Judah.* JSOTSup 276. Sheffield. Sheffield Academic Press.

Lemaire, André

1998 Les formules de datation en Palestine au premier millénaire avant J.-C. Pp. 53–82 in *Temps vécu, temps pensé: Actes de la table ronde du 15 novembre 1997 organisé par l'URA 1062,* ed. F. Briquel-Chatonnet and H. Lozachmeur. Études Sémitiques. Paris: Maisonneuve.

Lemaire, André, and Vernus, P.

1983 L'ostracon paléo-hébreu no. 6 de Tell Qudeirat (Qadesh-Barnéa). Pp. 302–26 in *Fontes atque Pontes: Eine Festgabe für Hellmut Brunner,* ed. M. Görg. Wiesbaden: Harrassowitz.

Levy, T. E.; Adams, R. B.; Hauptmann, A.; Prange, M.; Schmitt-Strecker, S.; and Najjar, M.

2002 Early Bronze Age Metallurgy: A Newly Discovered Copper Manufactory in Southern Jordan. *Antiquity* 76: 425–37.

Mazar, Amihai

2007 Precarious Scholarship: Problems with Proposing That the Seal of Yzbl Was Queen Jezebel's Response. ASOR web site: www.asor.org/mazar.htm.

Millard, Allan

1999 Owners and Users of Hebrew Seals. *ErIsr* 26 (Frank Moore Cross Volume): 129*–33*.

Na'aman, Nadav

2006 Three Notes on the Aramaic Inscription from Tel Dan. Pp. 173–86 in *Ancient Israel's History and Historiography: The First Temple Period.* Winona Lake, IN: Eisenbrauns.

Pardee, Dennis

1997 Gezer Calendar. P. 222 in *The Context of Scripture,* ed. W. Hallo and K. L. Younger. Leiden: Brill.

Pollock, Sheldon

2006 Response for Third Session: Power and Culture beyond Ideology and Identity. Pp. 277–87 in *Margins of Writing, Origins of Cultures: New Approaches to Writing and Reading in the Ancient Near East,* ed. S. Sanders. Chicago: Oriental Institute.

2007 *The Language of the Gods in the World of Men: Sanskrit, Culture, and Power in Premodern India.* Berkeley: University of California Press.

Reich, Ronny; Shukron, Eli; and Lernau, Omri

2007 Recent Discoveries in the City of David, Jerusalem. *IEJ* 57: 153–69.

Rollston, Christopher

2003 Non-Provenanced Epigraphs I: Pillaged Antiquities, Northwest Semitic Forgeries, and Protocols for Laboratory Tests. *Maarav* 10: 135–93.

2006 Scribal Education in Ancient Israel: The Old Hebrew Epigraphic Evidence. *BASOR* 344: 47–74.

Routledge, Bruce
2000 The Politics of Meshaʿ: Segmented Identities and State Formation in Iron Age Moab. *JESHO* 43: 221–56.
Sanders, Seth L.
2004 What Was the Alphabet For? The Rise of Written Vernaculars and the Making of Israelite National Literature. *Maarav* 11: 25–56.
forthcoming *The Invention of Hebrew.* Champaign-Urbana, IL: University of Illinois Press.
Sanders, Seth L., ed.
2006 *Margins of Writing, Origins of Cultures: New Approaches to Writing and Reading in the Ancient Near East.* Chicago: Oriental Institute.
Sass, Benjamin
1988 *The Genesis of the Alphabet and Its Development in the Second Millennium B.C.* Ägypten und Altes Testament 13. Wiesbaden: Harrassowitz.
Smith, Mark S.
2007 Recent Study of Israelite Religion in Light of the Ugaritic Texts. Pp. 1–26 in *Ugarit at Seventy-Five*, ed. K. L. Younger. Winona Lake, IN: Eisenbrauns.
Tappy, Ron E.; McCarter, P. Kyle, Jr.; Lundberg, Marilyn; and Zuckerman, Bruce
2006 An Abecedary of the Mid-Tenth Century B.C.E. from the Judaean Shephelah. *BASOR* 344: 5–46.
Warner, Michael
2002 Publics and Counter-Publics. *Public Culture* 14: 49–90.
Wilks, Ivor
1968 The Transmission of Islamic Learning in the Western Sudan. Pp. 162–97 in *Literacy in Traditional Societies*, ed. J. Goody. Cambridge: Cambridge University Press.
Wimmer, Stefan
2006 Egyptian Hieratic Writing in the Levant in the First Millennium B.C. *Abgadiyat* 1: 23–28.
Younger, K. Lawson
2007a The Late Bronze Age/Iron Age Transition and the Origins of the Arameans. Pp. 131–74 in *Ugarit at Seventy-Five*, ed. K. L. Younger. Winona Lake, IN: Eisenbrauns.
2007b Neo-Assyrian and Israelite History in the Ninth Century: The Role of Shalmaneser III. Pp. 243–77 in *Understanding the History of Ancient Israel*, ed. H. G. M. Williamson. Proceedings of the British Academy 143. Oxford: Oxford University Press.
Younger, K. Lawson, ed.
2007 *Ugarit at Seventy-Five.* Winona Lake, IN: Eisenbrauns.

The Tel Zayit Abecedary in (Social) Context

David M. Carr
Union Theological Seminary, New York

I suggest we develop a theory and an explanatory apparatus open enough to allow us to be surprised *by the past*
– S. Pollock, "Power and Culture beyond Ideology and Identity"

On one level, the Tel Zayit Abecedary is a modest find – just 22 letters barely visible on a stone set in a 10th-century wall. Yet on another level, as the original publishers of the inscription have stressed, the Tel Zayit Abecedary is very important. It stands as the most substantial inscription yet to be found in a stratified 10th-century archaeological context with links to the highland peoples of Judah and Israel. The fact that the inscription is an abecedary means that it contains examples of all the letters of the alphabet, thus providing an important comparison point for other, less datable inscriptions. Yet this essay will not focus on the development of the script itself. Instead, I use the script of the inscription as a pointer to broader developments in early Israelite writing.

To be sure, this kind of enterprise is not without risks. One could object that a small inscription of this sort, lacking as it does any grammatical constructions or identifiable words, cannot be the basis for broader theories about writing and literacy. Nevertheless, building particularly on Christopher Rollston's work on paleographical evidence for scribal schools in ancient Israel (Rollston 2006), I suggest that the Tel Zayit Abecedary may provide tantalizing data for the emergence of a broader system of writing and education in the hill country of 10th-century Canaan. Indeed, read in an admittedly maximalist way, this small inscription may provide important evidence for the emergence of broader, centralized social structures in early Israel as well.

Scripts and Broader Social Systems

A key presupposition in such a maximalist reading is the idea that standardized scripts of the sort seen in the inscription are created and preserved in broader social contexts, usually broader political systems.[1] People do not naturally write letter characters in the same form. Such standard letter forms must be taught in some kind of educational system spanning space and time. This educational system may not feature dedicated buildings and professional teachers – "schools" as one might conceive them today. Yet for a system successfully to transmit the same alphabet to students in widely divergent locations, it must have a certain ongoing shape to it, one that allows the transmission of detailed graphic knowledge to various individuals. For example, with an alphabet used simply for labels on private objects, one sees the kind of script variation typical of early alphabetic inscriptions on arrowheads and bowls. Standardized script, in contrast, marks a person's writing as "competent" in a broader social system, especially in scribal contexts, in which writing was one's craft.

Indeed, the *form* of the script often was viewed as an essential part of a broader and holy script-language that educated people had mastered. For this reason, most developed scribal systems of the ancient world started with sustained training in writing, whether cuneiform lists, hieratic signs, or abecedaries. This stage was the foundation of ancient scribal training – the learning not just of signs but also of particular forms of signs that distinguished the given scribal system. Moreover, these systems were successful enough in teaching particular letter forms that the forms of signs have been and can be used as important indicators of the date and provenance of otherwise undatable and unprovenanced inscriptions (Rollston 1999; 2006: 50–58).

As Ryan Byrne has pointed out, this focus on the craft of script standardization stands in complete contrast to the lack of care typical of writing in a culture in which print or other technology has made script standardization both easy and obsolete as a social marker. With a computer, one can achieve perfect script and nearly perfect spelling without going through the laborious processes of training formerly expended to achieve both (Byrne 2007: 4). As a result, penmanship often is no longer an index of one's level of education or professionalism. In ancient script cultures, however, the art of writing was a crucial component of the craft

1. There are some exceptions (for example, networks of monasteries), but most frequently the broader social context is, at least initially, a broader political system uniting diverse peoples.

of the professional scribe, and great care was taken in teaching and preserving that craft.

Byrne has also performed an important service in reviewing the data for scribal variability in early Iron Age Israel. In his exploration of the social location of textuality in the Iron I–Iron IIA periods, he notes the lack of standardization of key indexes of scribal textuality, such as the order of letters in abecedaries, placement of letters, and formation of letters. Building on Christopher Rollston's work on Hebrew scripts from the Iron IIB period, Byrne notes the contrast between such variability in early Iron Age textual remains and the standardization typical of the Iron IIB period. For him, this contrast is one indicator of the probable sponsorship, during the early Iron Age, of scribal textuality by individual patrons. There was no state at this point, but there were prestigious sponsors who came to value small inscriptions on their arrowheads, votive offerings, and so on (Byrne 2007: 17–23).

Meanwhile, Seth Sanders has built on the work of Rollston and others in a different way by suggesting that the standardization of script and literary language evident in later Hebrew inscriptions represents an important social phenomenon: the emergence of state structures that articulate and address the older social formation of "people" – that is, a group defined more by tribal affiliation than by connection to a specific territory or town. As Daniel Fleming most recently and thoroughly demonstrated, this formation of a tribal "people" had existed for far longer; we can see leaders dealing with various peoples in texts from the Mari archives, for example, and the Merneptah inscription mentions the "people" of Israel (Fleming 2004). Nevertheless, those are texts written by scribes in Egyptian or the Akkadian lingua franca about tribal peoples of the Bronze Age. What distinguishes Hebrew literature or the earlier literature of Ugarit, according to Sanders, is the development of a particular, standardized form of the alphabet to give a textual voice to a *local* language of a people. Previously, textual creations of this sort had to be voiced in a lingua franca created in another cultural center, especially Mesopotamia (the original home of literary Akkadian, the lingua franca of the Bronze Age Levant). But Sanders argues that we can see at Ugarit and in preexilic Israel the creation of literary vernacular literatures in specific alphabetic scripts that *distinguish* those local peoples from others around them (Sanders 2004).

This ancient link of script to people forms an interesting contrast to more modern processes discussed by Benedict Anderson in his evocative 1983 book, *Imagined Communities*.[2] There he argues that modern "nations"

2. Seth Sanders himself notes links of his ideas to Anderson's (see especially Sanders 2004: 30–31).

were built, to some extent, on preexisting communities of language that emerged with the creation of reading publics for newly formed print languages. Before this development, the vast majority of people spoke a fluid range of dialects not easily categorized into contemporary divisions, such as our "French," "German," or "English." Nevertheless, Anderson argues that publishers using the printing press helped promote specific print languages (that could represent a range of spoken dialects), thus creating an expanding corpus of print literature to appeal to a growing readership who would later identify themselves as "French," "German," or "English" on the basis of their shared print languages. Thus the use of print versions of vernacular languages by capitalist publishers helped create the precondition for the later formation of nation-states defined, in part, by these print-linguistic communities.

Anderson himself contrasts this more contemporary dynamic with the dynamic seen in earlier, more hierarchical script cultures, in which scribe-readers were "tiny literate reefs on top of vast illiterate oceans" (Anderson 1991: 15). Most members of ancient cultures had no opportunity to read and write, nor were societal resources devoted to broad teaching of literacy of any kind (Clanchy 1983; Graff 1981; 1987). In the absence of the printing press and the capitalist creation of communities of language, the linking of diverse ancient groups often happened by way of specific elites in those groups receiving a common education. This education created a culturally homogeneous leadership group who then served as the glue joining disparate groups together and administering the kingdom.

In this context, it is important to recognize that this ancient education, even alphabetic education, generally included far more than just learning to read and write a script. Some scholars have mistakenly assumed that the task of learning an alphabet would have taken no more than a few days or weeks.[3] This assumption is wrong on multiple counts. First, the idea that one can gain truly functional alphabetic competence quickly is a myth. Empirical studies of this process have shown that it takes years to gain expertise, especially with an early Semitic alphabet such as the almost completely consonantal one from Tel Zayit (Sanders 2004: 40; Rollston 2006: 48–49). Second, the learning of writing and reading in the ancient world was part of a broader scribal education in which the student learned to read, recite, and memorize a broader corpus of writings (Carr 2005: 3–109, 177–99).

Sometimes, as in the case of the Sumero-Akkadian system, students invested large portions of their time memorizing lists of signs and words before proceeding to literary works, such as Gilgamesh or Hammurapi. At other times, as in the case of cuneiform alphabetic education at Ugarit, stu-

3. For several examples, see Rollston 2006: 48.

dents appear to have moved straight from the learning of writing through abecedaries to working with texts written in the Ugaritic cuneiform alphabetic script. Even in Amarna Egypt, scribes using Akkadian to communicate with officials in Syria–Canaan learned their craft through a combination of cuneiform sign lists and a small corpus of Akkadian literary compositions (Edzard 1988; Artzi 1990; Izre'el 1997). In these cases and others, the learning of an ancient sign system was but one part of an educational process aimed at a knowledge that usually included mastery – oral, written, and memorized – of major texts written in the particular sign system. Ancient education of this sort was *not* focused on a narrower "literacy" defined by basic competence in reading and writing, which is often presumed in debates about the extent of literacy in ancient cultures such as Israel.

In sum, past work on Iron Age paleography and ancient education has shown various ways in which no standardized script is an island (to paraphrase John Donne). Instead, a standardized script is a pointer to a broader scribal system that developed and maintained the writing of specific letter forms, often in particular ways. As a result, a complete abecedary such as the Tel Zayit Inscription is valuable beyond what it tells us about paleographic developments. It is a potential pointer to emergent educational and sociopolitical formations to which we otherwise lack access.

Prologue: From Ugaritic to the Phoenician Writing System and Its Spread

Seth Sanders correctly points to the Ugaritic cuneiform alphabet as the first clear standardization of the alphabet for local literary purposes, but this alphabet did not survive the city's destruction around 1200 B.C.E. Moreover, the Ugaritic script, being *cuneiform*, partook of a broader tendency in the Bronze Age to use cuneiform for the sort of literary-scribal education discussed above. Whether in Egyptian Amarna, Syrian Emar, or even at Ugarit itself, scholarly elites across the ancient Near East were educated in local forms of the Sumero-Akkadian cuneiform tradition. They memorized local forms of the cuneiform sign lists and learned a small handful of Akkadian literary texts, such as the Epic of Gilgamesh or the Adapa Epic (Carr 2005: 47–61; Byrne 2007: 6–17). Meanwhile, from around 2000 B.C.E. onward, variable forms of the alphabet had been used mostly as a notation device, for labeling arrowheads and votive offerings, and for writing graffiti.[4] Sometime during the 14th century, Ugaritic scribes created a cuneiform version of the alphabet, standardized it, and

4. For a survey of the inscriptions, see Sass 1988. For more recent discussions, see especially Sanders 2004: 31–33 and Byrne 2007: 17–23.

used it to write a rich corpus of local literary texts. Yet even here, the hegemony of cuneiform writing was not broken. After all, the Ugaritic alphabet was an adaptation of cuneiform writing, Ugaritic scribes continued to learn and copy Akkadian texts, and the scribes do not appear to have translated Akkadian texts into their alphabetic cuneiform (or vice versa).[5]

In the 11th century, however, we begin to see the emergence in Phoenicia of a standardized, noncuneiform alphabetic script, along with its use in more extended royal inscriptions, such as the ʾAḥiram and Yeḥimilk inscriptions. Cuneiform as a medium for literary education, even alphabetic cuneiform, is out. In its place comes the Phoenician script series, used both in Phoenicia and – as evident at Tel Zayit, for example – elsewhere.

As suggested above, this standardized script is but the tip of a textual iceberg, even if – in the case of Phoenicia – we can only speculate on the existence of materials to which we have no access. Sadly, extended texts in the Phoenician and later alphabetic scripts typically were written on papyrus or parchment, materials that were far more perishable than the clay on which both Akkadian and Ugaritic alphabetic texts were written. As a result, the data for Iron Age alphabetic textuality, particularly literary forms of Iron Age textuality, is much less plentiful than for Bronze Age cuneiform textuality, and the randomness of finds is far greater. This situation renders highly risky any judgments about the absence of certain kinds of texts based on their nondiscovery (or variations in their contents) so far. This point can be illustrated with the example of Israel. If we did not have the Hebrew Bible and were limited to the kind of inscriptional evidence for Israel that we have for Phoenicia, the only literary texts to which we would have access would be fragments, such as the Keteph Ḥinnon amulets and the (still unpublished) hymnic inscription from Kuntillet ʿAjrud. On this basis, we might (wrongly) conclude from silence that, essentially, Israel lacked any sophisticated literature.

Certainly, given what we know about other systems of textuality in which extended texts like the Phoenician ʾAḥiram and Yeḥimilk inscriptions were produced, it is probable that Phoenicia had a corpus of literature – literature that is no longer extant but faint echoes of which we see in the Bible. Furthermore, given Phoenicia's unusually close ties to Egypt, this (nonextant) literature probably reflected influence from the Egyptian literary-educational system. The narrator of the Story of Wenamun thought it plausible to depict an Egyptian songstress as being available to sing in the court at Byblos (2.68–69), and some Phoenician inscriptions show the adaptation (for different purposes) of the red-lettering system seen earlier in Egypt (Chantraine 1972: 12–15; Edwards and Edwards 1974; Lemaire and

5. Dietrich 1996. I cite some minor possible exceptions (Carr 2005: 55).

Delevault 1979: 9). One other indicator of the possible character of Phoenician literature is the character of the local alphabetic literature at Ugarit – fortunately written on less perishable materials and possibly analogous in some respects to whatever literature was developed in Phoenicia (Millard 1979: 616). Beyond these indicators, we have little information. It is highly probable *that* a text-supported, oral-written form of Phoenician education stands behind these longer inscriptions – probably education with some particular links to Egypt – but we cannot know on the basis of the available evidence just *what* literature was in this system.

In the early Iron Age, the Phoenician script was used by neighbors developing their own forms of textuality in their native languages, and this writing system likely was accompanied – at least at the outset – by an encounter with some kind of Phoenician literature. For example, well into the 9th century, Arameans, often hundreds of kilometers distant from Phoenicia, used forms of the Phoenician script (and occasionally the Phoenician language) to write their earliest display texts. We see this phenomenon in the Kilamuwa, Tell Fakhariyeh, and Bir-Hadad inscriptions. Though they later developed their own standardized, local forms of the Phoenician script, the initial adoption of the Phoenician script in distant areas of Aram points to other levels of probable Phoenician influence. We see specific indicators of this multilevel influence in, for example, the Bir-Hadad Inscription, which stands below a relief of the Tyrian god Melkart and contains formulaic parallels to Phoenician votive texts (Gibson 1975: 2).

Meanwhile, there is increasing evidence for the influence of the Phoenician system in areas of the Judean Shephelah bordering Philistia – evidence from sites including Gezer, Lachish, Beth-shemesh, Tell Batash, and Tel Zayit, under discussion here (Lemaire and Delevault 1979). The Phoenician characteristics are so predominant in these early inscriptions, such as the Gezer Calendar, that scholars have debated whether they are Phoenician or Hebrew. Of course, that the script of these texts is Phoenician (or close to it) does not mean they were undoubtedly written by Phoenicians any more than the writing of the Tell Fakhariyeh Inscription in an old form of the Phoenician script makes it a Phoenician product. Even the Kilamuwa Inscription, a predominantly Phoenician-language inscription written with Phoenician script, also shows linguistic signs (for example, בר in line 1) of its Aramaic context.

It is certainly possible that some of these early inscriptions in border areas between Israel and Phoenicia were produced by non-Israelites; but it is just as likely that many are examples of early Israelite adoption of the Phoenician version of the alphabetic writing system. We continue to see examples of this Phoenician script in other Iron II inscriptions from Israel, such as some inscribed 9th- to 8th-century sherds from Hazor, inscribed ivories from Samaria, and four inscriptions at Kuntillet ʿAjrud (Lemaire and Delevault 1979: 27–28).[6] In each case, the writing and some orthography are Phoenician, reflecting the adopted scribal practice, but names, provenance, and/or other features in the inscriptions often mark them as (probably) Israelite texts.

The Emergence and Spread of the Hebrew Writing System

Sometime in the Iron Age, however, scribes in Israel and surrounding areas began to develop a standardized "inland" script that built on Phoenician prototypes but diverged in regular ways, thus suggesting the existence of an increasingly independent scribal-educational system. This development has been most fully documented in Christopher Rollston's work, which I have already discussed (Rollston 1999; 2006). Most of Rollston's work has focused on later Judean and Israelite scripts, from the 8th and 7th centuries, which show clear distinguishing marks from the alphabetic scribal traditions of Phoenicia on the one hand and the varied traditions of Aram on the other. In the wake of his and others' research, there is little doubt that late preexilic Israel and Judah had an alphabetic scribal system with its own integrity vis-à-vis its neighbors.

That said, there is indirect evidence that this "inland" scribal system originated earlier, despite the fact that its isolation and independent development are best reflected in later scripts. For example, it is striking how much the later Iron Age inscriptions from both the Southern and Northern Kingdoms share a common script tradition. As Renz and others have shown, it is virtually impossible to identify major differences between the script series of Judah and Israel (Renz 1997). Though the two kingdoms appear as highly distinct and sometimes hostile entities in the biblical narrative, the epigraphic record suggests a shared scribal tradition, perhaps on the analogy of the related versions of the Sumero-Akkadian tradition found at Nippur, other cities in southern Iraq, and then later Babylonian, Assyrian, and other cities.

Where did this shared scribal tradition come from? Possibly, it represents a random variation that spread in the area; but this possibility is not yet an explanation. Alternatively, the shared alphabet (and associated

6. Volkmar Fritz also thought the Tell ʿOreme Inscription (Or [8]:1) might be Phoenician (Renz 1995: 132). Note also the inscription with Phoenician letters from Khirbet el-Mudeni, which is dated by Rainey to the late 9th/early 8th century (Rainey 2003) but by others to a later period.

scribal system) may have resulted from imposition by one of the two kingdoms on the other – perhaps the more powerful Northern Israelite Kingdom on its Southern neighbor, Judah. As already discussed, the teaching of a shared scribal system, including the craft of a standardized script, served as one way of forming a cohesive elite of bureaucrats and leaders, a "literate reef" on a diverse and illiterate "ocean" (as Anderson puts it), with this scribal elite helping to unite diverse peoples in a larger sociopolitical entity. This observation leads to another possibility: namely, that the shared script tradition in Judah and Israel is an indicator of a shared scribal system that emerged already in the 10th century, when biblical traditions depict both kingdoms as being ruled from Jerusalem by David and Solomon.

Another indicator of the possible early emergence of this inland script tradition is the 9th-century Meshaʿ Inscription, which shows multiple links to later Hebrew scribal textuality in its alphabet, phraseology, and language. Again, these shared features point to probable scribal links between Moab and Israel/Judah. To be sure, as Sanders points out, one could understand these similarities as merely reflecting the use – by Israel, Judah, Moab, and other nearby peoples – of an inland version of the Phoenician script that just happened to be shared by these neighboring peoples (Sanders 2004: 55–56). Once again, however, this hypothesis is not yet an explanation of why this particular standardized script tradition is found specifically in Moab, along with Judah, Israel, and the neighboring areas of Philistia and Edom.

In this case, the inscription itself may provide clues to the process of distribution of this inland script tradition. Significant portions of the stele (especially lines 3–7) describe how Moab achieved liberation from Israel. Significantly, the stele focuses on Moab's former domination by and liberation from Northern Israel, while biblical traditions suggest that Moab – at least at an earlier point – was dominated by David in Judah (2 Sam 8:2, 12). One could interpret the "Hebrew" scribal features of the stele as a witness to the extension of a scribal system originating in the Northern Kingdom to Moab, which it once dominated (see 2 Kgs 1:1, 3:4–27). Alternatively, one might understand its shared scribal features with Judah and Israel as a reflection of yet earlier domination during the period of the United Monarchy. This latter hypothesis would explain not only the presence of the "Hebrew" script tradition in 9th-century Moab but also the presence of a similar script in later inscriptions from other areas described in biblical narratives as dominated by David, namely, Edom and Philistia (Naveh 1982: 100–105; Gitin, Dothan, and Naveh 1997). In either case, the Meshaʿ Inscription would be an example of Moabite scribes' using the standardized script and other aspects of the scribal system once used to link them to Israel to proclaim their liberation from the sociopolitical system that once dominated them.

To be sure, to speak of the possibility of a shared scribal tradition across parts of what the Bible describes as David's and Solomon's regional empire runs counter to the trend among many recent scholars to dismiss the idea that ancient Israel had an early state of the sort that would develop and spread a scribal textual-educational system. Where once there was consensus on the existence of a major Solomonic empire and concomitant Solomonic "enlightenment," some now see the biblical picture of the United Monarchy under David and Solomon as virtually a complete fiction, a projection of a "golden age" undermined by a reevaluation of archaeological data. The best recent assessments strike a middle ground. Certainly the biblical picture of a vast Solomonic empire and international Solomonic prestige partakes of the exaggeration typical of many ancient royal propaganda texts (Halpern 1996: 46–53), and the texts that most develop this picture are candidates for being relatively late additions to the Solomonic narrative (1 Kgs 5:1–14[4:20–34]). Nevertheless, the above epigraphic evidence for a spread of the Hebrew textual system to neighboring areas said to be dominated by Solomon (Moab and Philistia), the mention of the "House of David" as a historic state-dynasty in the Tel Dan Inscription, and the incipient urbanization in the 10th century and onward all join with the biblical narrative (which is relatively reliable on some important points for later periods) to suggest the emergence in the 10th century of an incipient state structure that extended power over some neighboring regions (Millard 1997: 27–28; Knoppers 1997; Miller 1997). This structure need not have educated and installed huge numbers of scribal bureaucrats. Nevertheless, the Bible does explicitly include a scribe in both David's and Solomon's court, thus paralleling the tendency in Egypt to include a head scribe among the king's head officials. The fact that these scribes are listed along with other major officials suggests that they were not just isolated retainers but played a similar leadership role in the state to the roles of other figures in the lists.[7]

In sum, even before we examine the Tel Zayit Inscription, there is evidence that some form of a distinctively Hebrew scribal system already emerged during the 10th century and was distributed across regions said to have been connected to David's and Solomon's kingdom: certainly Judah and Israel but also Moab and other regions reportedly conquered and dominated by David, such as Edom and Philistia. As discussed above,

7. On this suggestion, compare with Byrne (2007: 22) on David's scribe. In this respect, I find Byrne's position vis-à-vis Iron I more plausible than his arguments vis-à-vis Iron IIA.

some Israelite scribes appear to have continued to use the Phoenician script later in the Iron Age, so the distinctively Hebrew script and writing system did not completely replace its earlier counterpart. Nevertheless, by the 8th and 7th centuries the "Hebrew" script and writing system was dominant across Judah and Israel, while Phoenician writing was the exception. Let us turn now to see what the Tel Zayit Inscription might have to tell us about the situation in the 10th-century Judean Shephelah.

The Tel Zayit Inscription and Its Implications

First and foremost, the Tel Zayit Inscription appears to attest an intermediate state of scribal standardization. On the one hand, its script is standardized, representing either the Phoenician script or an inland script already on its way toward the distinctive features seen more clearly in the Moabite and later Israelite and Judean inscriptions. On the other hand, the alphabet follows several alternative letter orders, some with parallels in other abecedaries – for example, *ḥet-zayin* (at ʿIzbet Ṣarṭah) and *pe-ʿayin* (ʿIzbet Ṣarṭah, Kuntillet ʿAjrud and several biblical acrostics) – and some letter orders (especially *lamed-kap*, a possible error) that are not paralleled elsewhere (Tappy et al. 2006: 26; Byrne 2007: 4–5, 21). These alternative letter orders – especially the orders that are paralleled in other inscriptions – show that the abecedary at this early point was still in somewhat of a state of flux. Whatever scribal system had emerged, it had not yet achieved the standardization of alphabetic order evident in much later abecedaries and the acrostics of the Hebrew Bible.

The debate between Kyle McCarter and Christopher Rollston has implications for one's interpretation of the elements of the inscription that appear to reflect scribal standardization. If McCarter is correct, the Tel Zayit Inscription already attests the development of an "inland" version of the Phoenician script, a version later attested more broadly in various Hebrew, Moabite, and other inscriptions. Thus the Tel Zayit Inscription would be important evidence for the emergence – by the late 10th century – of a distinctively Hebrew scribal tradition, a tradition that was part of a broader literary system for shaping bureaucratic elites. As such, it would combine with other evidence discussed above (the distribution of the Hebrew script across areas associated with David's and Solomon's United Monarchy) for the emergence of a distinctively Hebrew scribal system in the 10th century.

Yet even if the Tel Zayit Abecedary is indistinguishably Phoenician in form, as suggested by Christopher Rollston, the inscription still testifies to the initial adoption in 10th-century Judah–Israel of an originally Phoenician script tradition, probably along with some other elements of the

Phoenician literary system. As such, the Tel Zayit inscription stands alongside evidence in the Bible itself to other ways in which Phoenicia was linked to David's and particularly Solomon's kingdom, as in the building of the Jerusalem temple and royal palace, for example. Moreover, the location of the inscription at Tel Zayit suggests use of the Phoenician script well outside Jerusalem, in a town situated on the frontier of Judah and Philistia at the nexus of multiple communication routes.

In either case, I am not arguing here that the Tel Zayit Inscription proves the existence of a magnificent Solomonic empire extending from the Nile to the Euphrates and enjoying a literary golden age. The presence of the abecedary does not prove general education or universal literacy. Instead, recent work by Stager, Zevit, and others has refined our sense of the sort of Solomonic kingdom that might have existed and the way to recognize it if it did (Schäfer-Lichtenberger 1996; Stager 2003). Other work on ancient textuality has clarified such a kingdom's various functions and identified as anachronistic many concepts – for example, universal literacy – that some scholars of antiquity have applied to the ancient record. Indeed, we should not be picturing a Solomonic enlightenment with universal literacy in 10th-century Israel. Instead, a combination of evidence, including now the Tel Zayit Abecedary, suggests that late 10th-century Israel had an emergent state structure, one that included borrowing or adaptation of the Phoenician alphabetic scribal system in some administrative centers and the learning of this system by a limited number of officials.

Rethinking 10th-Century Judean-Israelite Scribalism

I conclude by setting these findings in a broader scholarly perspective. Earlier I alluded to doubt among biblical scholars about the existence of a Davidic-Solomonic monarchy in general and an associated literary-scribal system in particular. For example, Jamieson-Drake, in his oft-cited dissertation, asserted, "There is little evidence that Judah began to function as a state at all prior to the tremendous increases in population, building, production, centralization and specialization which began to appear in the 8th century" (Jamieson-Drake 1991: 139–40). He went on to conclude that "professional administrators were trained in Jerusalem, and only in Jerusalem. Further, specialized training in administrative skills was apparently needed on a broad basis only in the 8th–7th centuries, when the administrative demands of managing a regionally interdependent economic network would have required a concomitant quantum leap in regional communications" (Jamieson-Drake 1991: 148). These ideas found increasingly broad acceptance among other scholars, such as Israel Finkelstein and Neil Silberman, who, in their 2001 popular book, *The Bible Unearthed*, noted the absence of evidence for a "centrally administered state" in 10th-century Judah and asserted, "Not a single trace of tenth century Judahite literary activity has been found. . . . In light of these findings, it is now clear that Iron Age Judah enjoyed no precocious golden age" (Finkelstein and Silberman 2001: 235, 238).

These perspectives on the nonexistence of a Davidic-Solomonic kingdom and associated literary writing have influenced reconstructions of the history of Israelite literature. For example, in his 2004 publication, *How the Bible Became a Book*, William Schniedewind said in his discussion of the Davidic-Solomonic kingdom, "Writing did not play an important enough role in early Israelite society to warrant writing down these songs and stories, proverbs and parables. That time, however, would come in the eighth century" (Schniedewind 2004: 63). And lest I be accused of being unfair to colleagues, let me add one more quotation: "Jamieson-Drake's thorough analysis of material culture associated with writing indicates that we do not see in the tenth century any significant concentration of population, [etc.] that would point to a state apparatus requiring extensive written communication." This last quotation comes from my own discussion of the Davidic-Solomonic period in my book on Genesis published in 1996 (Carr 1996: 221).

The discovery of the Tel Zayit Inscription proves just how dangerous it can be to base arguments about early ancient history on *gaps* in the historical record. Therefore, I believe that other scholars and I were ill advised in reading too much into the relative absence of data for writing in the 10th century B.C.E. So much has depended on the expectations of scholars interpreting the evidence. Researchers have decided what we *should* have found in the archaeological record, were there a Solomonic kingdom with an emergent literature. Then, because their relatively unscrutinized expectations have gone unfulfilled, they have decided there was no Solomonic kingdom or associated literature.

We must be equally careful, however, not to plug the Tel Zayit Inscription into similarly unsupported assumptions about the existence of a full state structure in 10th-century Israel, the existence of an extensive Solomonic empire, or the presence of a "Solomonic enlightenment" featuring something like universal literacy. Indeed, it remains possible that the Tel Zayit Inscription only reflects the fairly isolated presence of a scribe educated in the Phoenician system in a border region between the inland tribes of Judah and Israel and the cities of Phoenicia. Nevertheless, I have argued here that the presence of the abecedary at Tel Zayit probably tells us more than that about the emergence of alphabetic scribalism in early Israel. In the initial report about the inscription, Tappy mentions that this town may well have been a local center for the Naḥal Guvrin-District 4 administrative area (Tappy et al. 2006: 6–7). If so, this inscription could be evidence for the concentration of writing in similar administrative centers of ancient Judah. Furthermore, Tel Zayit is also small enough and distant enough from Jerusalem that the presence of this inscription there might be taken as testimony of more widespread writing across more far-flung and minor administrative centers of Judah than Jamieson-Drake and others supposed.

In the reconstruction of ancient history, we are limited to suppositions based on scraps and tatters, especially for societies such as Judah and Israel in which the most commonly used writing media, papyrus and parchment, were perishable. As a result, we face two major risks in interpreting finds such as the inscription at Tel Zayit. On the one hand, we may be tempted to overinterpret the find by too quickly fitting meager data into preexisting schemes, such as the idea of a Solomonic enlightenment or widespread scribalism. On the other hand, we also face the risk of overinterpreting gaps in the archaeological record by emphasizing the significance of the lack of inscriptions like the abecedary discovered at Tel Zayit, only to face difficulties when theories based on absence are undermined by new finds. The challenge as we continue to think about the Tel Zayit Abecedary and other finds that will surely emerge over the coming years is to keep open to being surprised by the data, as suggested by the epigraph at the outset of this essay. Given the meager and often problematic evidence for 10th-century Israel and Judah, it is a challenge indeed to find ways to be "surprised by the past," as Sheldon Pollock urges. Nevertheless, the Tel Zayit Inscription offers a major opportunity to do just this.

Bibliography

Anderson, B.

1991 *Imagined Communities: Reflections on the Origin and Spread of Nationalism.* Rev. ed. New York: Verso. [Original 1983]

Artzi, P.

1990 Studies in the Library of the Amarna Archive. Pp. 139–56 in *Bar-Ilan Studies in Assyriology Dedicated to Pinḥas Artzi*, ed. J. Klein and A. Skaist. Ramat Gan: Bar-Ilan University Press.

Byrne, R.

2007 The Refuge of Scribalism in Iron I Palestine. *BASOR* 345: 1–31.

Carr, D. M.

1996 *Reading the Fractures of Genesis: Historical and Literary Approaches.* Louisville: Westminster John Knox.

2005 *Writing on the Tablet of the Heart: Origins of Scripture and Literature.* New York: Oxford University Press.

Chantraine, P.
1972 A propos du nom des Phéniciens et des noms de la pourpre. *Studii Classici* 14: 7–15.
Clanchy, M. T.
1983 Looking Back from the Invention of Printing. Pp. 7–22 in *Literacy in Historical Perspective*, ed. D. P. Resnick. Washington, DC: Library of Congress.
Dietrich, M.
1996 Aspects of the Babylonian Impact on Ugaritic Literature and Religion. Pp. 33–47 in *Ugarit, Religion and Culture: Proceedings of the International Colloquium on Ugarit, Religion and Culture, Edinburgh, July 1994*, ed. N. Wyatt et al. Münster: Ugarit Verlag.
Edwards, G. P., and Edwards, R. B.
1974 Red Letters and Phoenician Writings. *Kadmos* 13: 48–57.
Edzard, D. O.
1988 Amarna: Die literarische Texte. Pp. 27-33 in *Proceedings of the Ninth World Congress of Jewish Studies*. Jerusalem: World Union of Jewish Studies.
Finkelstein, I., and Silberman, N.
2001 *The Bible Unearthed: Archaeology's New Vision of Ancient Israel and the Origin of Its Sacred Texts*. New York: Free Press.
Fleming, D.
2004 *Democracy's Ancient Ancestors: Mari and Early Collective Governance*. Cambridge: Cambridge University Press.
Gibson, J. C. L.
1975 *Textbook of Syrian Semitic Inscriptions*. Oxford: Clarendon.
Gitin, S.; Dothan, T.; and Naveh, J.
1997 A Royal Dedicatory Inscription from Ekron. *IEJ* 47: 1–16.
Graff, H. J.
1981 Literacy, Jobs and Industrialization: The Nineteenth Century. Pp. 232–60 in *Literacy and Social Development in the West: A Reader*, ed. H. J. Graff. Cambridge: Cambridge University Press.
1987 *The Legacies of Literacy: Continuities and Contradictions in Western Culture and Society*. Bloomington: Indiana University Press.
Halpern, B.
1996 The Construction of the Davidic State: An Exercise in Historiography. Pp. 44–75 in *The Origins of the Ancient Israelite States*, ed. V. Fritz and P. R. Davies. JSOTSup 228. Sheffield: Sheffield Academic Press.
Izre'el, S.
1997 *The Amarna Scholarly Tablets*. Cuneiform Monographs 9. Gröningen: Styx.
Jamieson-Drake, D. W.
1991 *Scribes and Schools in Monarchic Judah: A Socio-Archeological Approach*. JSOTSup 109. Sheffield: Almond.
Knoppers, G. N.
1997 The Vanishing Solomon: The Disappearance of the United Monarchy from Recent Histories of Ancient Israel. *JBL* 116: 19–44.

Lemaire, A., and Delevault, B.
1979 Les inscriptions phéniciennes de la Palestine. *Rivista di Studi Fenici* 7: 19–39.

Millard, A.
1979 The Ugaritic and Canaanite Alphabets: Some Notes. *Ugarit-Forschungen* 11: 613–16.
1997 Assessing Solomon: History or Legend? Pp. 25–29 in *The Age of Solomon: Scholarship at the Turn of the Millennium*, ed. L. K. Handy. Leiden: Brill.

Miller, J. M.
1997 Separating the Solomon of History from the Solomon of Legend. Pp. 1–24 in *The Age of Solomon: Scholarship at the Turn of the Millennium*, ed. L. K. Handy. Leiden: Brill.

Naveh, J.
1982 *Early History of the Alphabet.* Jerusalem: Magnes / Leiden: Brill.

Pollock, S.
2006 Response for Third Session: Power and Culture beyond Ideology and Identity. Pp. 277–86 in *Margins of Writing, Origins of Cultures*, ed. S. Sanders. Chicago: University of Chicago Press.

Rainey, A. F.
2003 The New Inscription from Khirbet el-Mudeiyineh. *IEJ* 52: 81–86.

Renz, J.
1995 *Handbuch der althebräische Epigraphik.* Darmstadt: Wissenschaftliche.
1997 *Schrift und Schreibertradition: Eine paläographische Studie zum Kulturgeschichtlichen Verhältnis von israelitischem Nordreich und Südreich.* Wiesbaden: Harrassowitz.

Rollston, C.
1999 *The Script of Hebrew Ostraca of the Iron Age: 8th–6th Centuries BCE.* Ph.D. dissertation. Johns Hopkins University.
2006 Scribal Education in Ancient Israel: The Old Hebrew Epigraphic Evidence. *BASOR* 344: 47–74.

Sanders, S.
2004 What Was the Alphabet For? The Rise of Written Vernaculars and the Making of Israelite National Literature. *Maarav* 11: 25–56.

Sass, B.
1988 *The Genesis of the Alphabet and Its Development in the Second Millenium B.C.* Wiesbaden: Harrassowitz.

Schäfer-Lichtenberger, C.
1996 Sociological and Biblical Views of the Early State. Pp. 78–105 in *The Origins of the Ancient Israelite States*, ed. V. Fritz and P. R. Davies. JSOTSup 228. Sheffield: Sheffield Academic Press.

Schniedewind, W.
2004 *How the Bible Became a Book.* Cambridge: Cambridge University Press.

Stager, L.
2003 The Patrimonial Kingdom of Solomon. Pp. 63–74 in *Symbiosis, Symbolism and the Power of the Past: Canaan, Ancient Israel, and Their Neighbors*

from the Late Bronze Age through Roman Palaestina, ed. W. G. Dever and S. Gitin. Winona Lake, IN: Eisenbrauns.

Tappy, Ron E.; McCarter, P. Kyle; Lundberg, Marilyn J.; and Zuckerman, Bruce
2006 An Abecedary of the Mid-Tenth Century B.C.E. from the Judaean Shephelah. *BASOR* 344: 5–46.

Index of Authors

Abou-Assaf, A. 66
Adams, R. B. 106
Aharoni, Y. 1, 49, 81
Albright 67
Albright, W. F. 67, 80
Alexandre, Y. 78
Amiran, R. 1
Anderson, B. 19, 108, 115–116, 121
Anzaldúa, G. 1, 18
Artzi, P. 117
Aufrecht, W. E. 66
Avigad, N. 103

Bakhtin, M. 19
Barth, F. 19, 22
Basu, P. 14
Baumgartner, W. 63
Beech, J. R. 68
Beidelman, T. O. 14
Ben-Amos, D. 14
Ben Zvi, E. 36
Berent, I. 70
Bordreuil, P. 46, 66, 99
Bosman, A. M. T. 68
Boyarin, D. 108
Brunner, H. 67
Bunimovitz, S. 4, 6–9, 12, 45, 81
Byrne, B. 61
Byrne, R. 71, 99, 102, 106, 114–115, 117, 122–123

Carr, D. M. x, 61, 116–118, 125
Chantraine, P. 118
Chen, C. 67
Clanchy, M. T. 116
Cogan, M. 33, 36
Cohen, A. 14, 17, 19
Cohen, M. E. 100
Cohen, R. 49
Cole, J. W. 16
Coleman, S. 14
Conder, C. R. 1
Crenshaw, J. L. 68, 72
Cross, F. M. 46, 48–49, 51, 53–54, 56, 65, 73, 78, 80, 84–88

Dagan, Y. 1
Darnell, J. C. 72
Davis, N. Z. 103
Deflem, M. 15
Degen, R. 64
Delevault, B. 119–120
Demsky, A. 49
Deutsch, R. 46
Dietrich, M. 118
Diringer, D. 49
Donnan, H. 17, 19, 21–24, 35
Donne, J. 117
Donner, H. 76
Dorsey, D. 11
Dothan, T. 121
Duisch, J. 14

Eade, J. 14–15
Edelstein, G. 45
Edwards, G. P. 118
Edwards, R. B. 118
Edzard, D. O. 117
Efrat, E. 23
Ehri, L. 68–69

Fayol, M. 69
Finkelstein, I. 124–125
Fleming, D. 105, 115
Fox, R. G. 12
Frahm, E. 33, 36
Freedman, D. N. 49, 65, 80
Friedrich, J. 64
Fritz, V. 120
Frost, R. 61, 70

Gagarin, M. 106
Gal, Z. 81
Galil, G. 37
Garr, R. 65–66
Gaster, T. H. 49
Gennep, A. van 13, 18
George, A. 67
Geva, E. 69
Gibson, J. C. L. 119
Gitin, S. 8, 33, 121
Giveon, R. 49
Gogel, S. L. 64
Goldwasser, O. 106
Gough, P. B. 69
Graeber, D. 100
Graff, H. J. 116
Graham-White, A. 14, 40
Grant, E. 49
Griffith, P. L. 69
Guillemin, A. M. 71

Habermas, J. 108
Hackett, J. A. 48, 53
Halpern, B. 122
Hamilton, G. J. 104
Haran, M. 72
Harris, W. V. 71
Harris, Z. S. 65
Havelock, E. A. 71
Hawley, R. 105
Heltzer, M. 46
Henderson, E. 68
Heslinga, M. W. 23
Hess, R. S. 62–63
Hoftijzer, J. 63
Horowitz, W. 102
Horsman, M. 19, 21
Huyssteen, J. W. van 19

Izre'el, S. 117

Jamieson-Drake, D. W. 67–68, 124–126
Janssen, J. J. 67
Janssen, R. 67
Japhet, S. 31, 40
Jongeling, K. 63
Joüon, P. 64
Juel, C. 69

Kallner, R. B. 49
Kaufman, S. A. 66
Kavanagh, W. 18–19
Kelly, J. 105
Kelm, G. 28, 31, 33–34, 45, 81
Kessler, B. 61
Khalidi, W. 1
Kitchener, H. H. 1
Kletter, R. 106
Knoppers, G. N. 122
Kochavi, M. 49
Koehler, L. 63
Kopytoff, I. 19, 22–23

Landerl, K. 69
Lederman, Z. 4, 6–9, 12, 45, 81
Lee, S. Y. 67
Lemaire, A. 71, 101, 106, 118–120
Lernau, O. 103
Levin, I. 69–70
Levy, S. 45
Lundberg, M. 5, 74

Macalister, R. A. S. 80
Maravall, J. A. 19
Marshall, A. 19, 21
Mazar, A. 8, 28, 30–31, 33–36, 45, 81, 103
McCarter, P. K., Jr. x, 46–47, 49, 73, 77, 81–83, 88, 97, 102, 104, 123
McDowell, A. G. 67
Milik, J. T. 46
Millard, A. R. 66, 103, 119, 122
Miller, J. M. 122
Mitchell, H. 14
Moran, W. L. 65

Naʾaman, N. 33, 107
Naveh, J. 49, 53, 73, 78, 80, 86–89, 121
Niditch, S. 61

O'Connor, M. 64, 66
Olmo Lete, G. del 63
Orden, G. C. van 68
Oshima, T. 102

Panitz-Cohen, N. 28, 30–31, 33–36
Pardee, D. 99–100
Peacock, J. 14
Peckham, B. 73, 77
Pollock, S. 101, 108, 113, 126
Pritchard, J. B. 48
Puech, E. 72

Rabinowitz, D. 22
Radovan, Z. 5
Rainey, A. F. 11, 36, 65, 120
Ravid, D. 70
Reich, R. 103
Renz, J. 120
Richgels, D. J. 68
Röllig, W. 64, 76
Rollston, C. A. x, 61, 63, 65, 67–68, 72–73, 77–78, 87–88, 97, 102, 113–116, 120, 123
Rosaldo, R. 18
Rosander, E. E. 14
Rosenberg, J. 2
Routledge, B. 107

Sader, H. 70
Sahlins, P. 17, 19, 22
Sallnow, M. J. 14–15, 22
Sanders, S. L. x, 71, 99, 102, 107–108, 115–117, 121
Sanmartín, J. 63
Sartre, J.-P. 19
Sass, B. 76, 103–104, 117
Schäfer-Lichtenberger, C. 124
Schniedewind, W. M. 61, 125
Schrag, C. 19
Segert, S. 64
Seymour, P. H. K. 61, 68–69
Share, D. L. 70
Shatil, E. 70
Shukron, E. 103
Silberman, N. 125
Skaff, A. 70
Smith, M. S. 99, 107
Stager, L. E. 49, 124
Stokes, M. 22, 35
Sudilovsky, J. 37
Sukenik, E. L. 49

Tadmor, H. 37
Tappy, R. E. ix–x, 3–4, 8, 10–11, 13, 16, 20, 23–25, 27–28, 31–34, 36, 45, 56, 62, 71–72, 81–83, 88, 97, 123, 125–126
Thevenin, M. 69
Tinney, S. 67
Toorn, K. van der 71
Totereau, C. 69
Treiman, R. 61, 69
Tropper, J. 64
Turner, E. 14
Turner, F. J. 23
Turner, V. 13–15, 18

Ussishkin, D. 4, 7–8, 35, 49
Uttal, D. H. 67

Vanstiphout, H. L. J. 67
Vaughn, A. G. 33
Veldhuis, N. 67
Vernus, P. 106

Waltke, B. 64
Warner, M. 108
Weber, D. 14–15
Weeks, S. 68, 72
Wilks, I. 105
Williamson, H. G. M. 36
Wilson, T. M. 17, 19, 21–24, 35
Wimmer, H. 69
Wimmer, S. 106
Wolf, E. R. 16

Yadin, Y. 81
Young, I. 63
Younger, K. L., Jr. 36, 105, 107

Zevit, Z. 65, 124

Index of Scripture

Joshua
15 23, 30, 37
15:11 31
15:33–44 11, 32, 35
15:35–36 11
15:37–41 11
15:42–44 11
15:45–47 35, 37

Judges
1:18 33

1 Samuel
5–6 33
5:6 36
7:14 33
17:52 33

2 Samuel
8:2 121
8:12 121

1 Kings
4:7 100
5:1–14[4:20–34] 122
6:37–38 101
6:38 101
8:2 101
15:16–22 19

2 Kings
1:1 121
3:4–27 121
8:22 30

2 Chronicles
21:10 30
26:6 31, 36
26:6–8 36
28 32
28:18 31

Isaiah
14:28–32 31

Jeremiah
10:11 65

Micah
1:10–16 32

Index of Topics

ʾAbbaʾ seal 49, 49 n. 10, 50, 52
 see also Revadim seal
ʿAbdaʾ Sherd Graffito 75
abecedary(-ies) 5 fig. 3, 10, 12, 28 fig. 10, 37, 45, 62–67, 67 n. 10, 71–72, 82, 102, 102 n. 9, 104, 107, 113–15, 117, 123–26
ʾAbibaʿl 76, 98
 Inscription 52 fig. 3, 75–76, 79, 82, 89
acrostics (biblical) 123
Adapa Epic 117
Adullam 11
Ahaz 27, 31–33
ʾAḥiram 74, 75–76, 98
 Inscription/Sarcophagus 51, 52 fig. 3, 74 fig. 3, 74–76, 82, 84 fig. 9, 86, 88–89, 118
 tomb-shaft graffito 52
ʾAmal, Tel 2 fig. 1, 45 n. 1, 53, 83
 see also ʿAṣi, Tell el-
Amarna (Age/Letters) 21, 65 n. 6, 117
Amaziah 27
American Schools of Oriental Research 1 n. 1
ʿAmman Statue Inscription 66
ʿAmman Citadel Inscription 56, 85 fig. 10, 86–87
Ammonite 66
Amorite(s) 105
Amurru 47 n. 3, 106
Arabesk 22 n. 14
Arabic, Classical 65–66
Arad 2 fig. 1, 28
 Ostraca 81, 101
Aram 119–20
Aramaic script 56, 73, 78
 early 85 fig. 10
Aramean(s) 105
ʿAreini, Tell el- 10, 23 n. 16, 24, 25 fig. 8
arrowheads 46, 47, 47 n. 3, 48, 48 n. 7, 49–54, 50 fig. 2, 84 fig. 9, 106, 114–15, 117
Asa 19
Ashdod 2 fig. 1, 25 fig. 8, 31, 33–37
Ashdod-yam 36
Ashkelon 2 fig. 1, 11, 25 fig. 8, 34, 36
Asia 105
Asia Minor 77
ʿAṣi, Tell el- 45 n. 1
 see also ʾAmal, Tel
Attica 71 n. 16
Ayalon, Valley of 10, 31
ʿAzarbaʿl Inscription 74, 79, 82
 see also Bronze ʿAzarbaʿal Inscription
Azekah 11, 23 n. 16, 25 fig. 8, 26, 32
 Inscription 33 n. 19
Azitawadda 77

Baal 98–99
Baasha 19
Babylon 38, 99
Baʿl Lebanon Inscription 55 fig. 4
Bar-Rakib Inscription 78
Batash, Tel 2 fig. 1, 8–9, 26, 28, 30–31, 33–34, 45 n. 1, 81, 83, 119
 see also Timnah
Beersheba 2 fig. 1
Beqaʿ 47 n. 3
Beth Guvrin Valley 1, 23 n. 16, 30
 see also Naḥal Guvrin
Bethlehem 11
Beth-shan 45 n. 1
Beth-shemesh 2 fig. 1, 4, 6–10, 11 n. 6, 17, 23 n. 16, 24, 25 fig. 8, 26–28, 32, 37, 45 n. 1, 81, 83, 119

Beth-shemesh *(cont.)*
Abecedary 102 n. 10
Ostracon/Inscription 49, 49 n. 9, 50, 52, 83
Bir-Hadad Inscription 55–56, 78, 85 fig. 10, 85–87, 119
Bornat, Tell 23 n. 16, 25 fig. 8, 26
Bronze ʿAzarbaʿl (Spatula) Inscription 73 fig. 2, 73–74, 89
see also ʿAzarbaʿl Inscription
Buddhism 105
Bul (month of) 101
bulla(s) 103, 103 n. 12
Byblian royal inscriptions/sequence/series 48, 51, 53, 88, 98
see also Phoenicia, Royal Inscriptions)
Byblos (Gebal) 2 fig. 1, 49 n. 7, 74–77, 80, 89, 98, 118

Canaan (Syria-) 4, 10, 12, 17, 18 n. 11, 21, 23 n. 15, 34, 45, 47–48, 80, 83, 97–99, 113, 117
caravan archive (Old Assyrian) 105
Carthage, gold pendant 55 fig. 4
Catalan borderlands 17
Central Processing Hypothesis 69 n. 14
Cerdanya Valley 17, 22 n. 14
China 71
City of David 103
coastal (type) pottery/forms 6–8, 8 n. 4, 30–31, 34
communitas 14–15, 14 n. 7
complex liminal zone 20, 20 fig. 6
copper smelting 106
core(s) (vs. periphery) 12–13, 13 fig. 4, 15–17, 18 n. 11, 19, 21–22, 23 n. 16, 24, 25 fig. 8, 26, 30–31, 33–35, 37–38
Crete 106 n. 15
curriculum 103-07
Cyprus 55 fig. 4, 77, 83

Dan 7
Damascus 2 fig. 1, 31
David(-ic) 97, 121–25, 122 n. 7, 123–24
see also City of David
deep orthography 69, 69 n. 14
diphthong contraction 47

Edom 121–22
Edomite script 49
education 113–14, 116–19
educational system 114, 120
Egypt 11–12, 67, 67 n. 11, 104, 117–19, 122
Egyptians 33
Ekron 2 fig. 1, 8–10, 25 fig. 8, 31–38
see also Miqne, Tel
El 99
Elah Valley 23 n. 16, 30, 38
El Amarna 65 n. 6
ʾEl-Ḫaḍr 52
arrowheads 84 fig. 9
ʾElibaʿl 75–76, 98
Inscription 52 fig. 3, 75, 82, 89
Emar 99, 107, 117
Eshtemoaʿ 2 fig. 1, 83
Ethiopians 33
Euphrates River 106, 124

Faraʿ (S), Tell el- 2 fig. 1, 83
Faynan 106
France 17, 22 n. 14, 103
fulcrum markets 34
functional literacy *see* literacy, functional

Galilee 78
gaming board 45 n. 1
Gath 10, 23 n. 16, 25 fig. 8, 26, 31–34, 36, 38
see also Ṣafi, Tell eṣ-
Gaza 2 fig. 1, 11, 25 fig. 8, 31–32, 35–36
Gebal *see* Byblos
Gedor 11
Gezer 2 fig. 1, 7, 20–21, 25 fig. 8, 33, 50–51, 54, 119

Gezer *(cont.)*
  Calendar 45 n. 1, 48–54, 50 fig. 2, 52 fig. 3, 56, 56 n. 12, 79 fig. 7, 80, 82, 82 n. 23, 84 fig. 9, 88, 97, 100–1, 103–4, 109, 119
Gibbethon 36
Gibeon 28
Gilgamesh, Epic of 116–17
Goded, Tel 11
Gozan Pedestal Inscription 56, 85 fig. 10, 87
graffito(-i) 45, 117
Greece 70, 106 n. 15
Greek script/language 54, 70
Guvrin Valley *see* Beth Guvrin Valley

Hadad Inscription 78
Hammurapi 99, 106, 116
Hatay Province 22 n. 14, 35 n. 20
Ḥazael 31
Ḥazaʾel Inscriptions 85 fig. 10, 87
Hazor 2 fig. 1, 80, 120
Hebrew (national) script 45, 47, 49, 51, 53–54, 56, 62, 83, 97, 115, 121, 123
Hebrew scribal system 122–23
Hebron 11
Heshbon (A1: 2) 65
Ḥesi, Tell el- 10, 24, 25 fig. 8
Hezekiah 32–33, 38
hieratic 106–7, 114
Hittite (hieroglyphic) 77
Honeyman Inscription 55 fig. 4, 77, 83, 88
Horse ornament 75 fig. 10
"House of David" 122

Imperial Aramaic 65
inland script (tradition/scribal system) 120–21, 123
Iraq 120
Islam 105
Israel 14 n. 7, 19, 62, 68, 79–80, 97–98, 100–4, 107, 109, 113, 115, 117–26
Israel *(cont.)*
  United Monarchy 6, 8–9, 62, 121–24
Italy 16, 71, 71 n. 16
ʾIttobaʿl 74, 76, 98
ʿIzbet Ṣarṭa 2 fig. 1, 102, 104, 123
  Ostracon 49, 49 n. 10, 50 fig. 2, 50–53, 84 fig. 9, 86 fig. 11, 86, 104

Jabneh/Jabneel 31
Japan 71
Jarmuth 11 n. 6
Jedur, Khirbet 11
Jehoshaphat 10, 31
Jerusalem 2 fig. 1, 7–10, 12, 25 fig. 8, 31, 33, 103 n. 12, 121, 124, 126
Jerusalem Corridor 23 n. 16
Joash 27
Jordan 106
Josiah 35
Judah, Kingdom of 1, 6–11, 14, 14 n. 7, 15, 17–18, 18 n. 11, 19–21, 26–28, 30–31, 31 n. 18, 32–38, 97, 103, 106, 113, 120–26
Judeideh, Tell 23 n. 16, 25 fig. 8, 26

Karatepe 77
  inscriptions 55 fig. 4, 77
kārum (merchant colony) 105
Kefar Veradim 2 fig. 1, 78
  Bowl/Inscription 78 fig. 6, 78, 82
Kemoshyat 99
Ketef Ḥinnom (amulets) 118
Kilamuwa Inscription 55–56, 78, 85 fig. 10, 86–87, 89, 119
Kiriath-jearim 28
Kition 77
  Bowl 77, 86, 87 fig. 12
Kuntillet ʿAjrud 106, 118, 120, 123
  inscriptions 98–99
  pithoi 56
  stone bowl 51, 56

Lachish (Valley) 1, 2 fig. 1, 4, 6–8, 10–11, 16 n. 8, 18, 23 n. 16, 24, 26–27, 30–32, 35, 37–38, 119

Lachish *(cont.)*
Bowl No. 1 49, 49 n. 8
Ewer 49, 49 n. 8, 52
Ostracon 49, 49 n. 8, 51
Latin 70
Lebanon 7
Levant 47, 61, 63, 68, 70, 72, 89, 99, 103, 107, 107 n. 17, 108–9, 115
Libnah 11, 25 fig. 8, 30, 37
limen 13, 16, 26
liminal zone 14 n. 7, 15, 16 fig. 5, 17–18, 18 n. 11, 19–24, 20 fig. 6, 25 fig. 8, 26, 28, 30–38
see also marginal zone
Linear Phoenician *see* Phoenician, linear
literacy 47–48, 61–63, 67–68, 70–72, 105, 113, 116–17, 124–25
functional 61–62
literary boundary 35
LMLK jars 31, 33–34
lunisolar (ritual) calendar 101
Luristan Bronze Jug 85 fig. 10

Malta Stele 55 fig. 4, 77
Manaḥat Sherd 49, 49 n. 10, 51
marginal zone/area 15, 18–21, 32, 38
see also liminal zone
Mari (archives) 106–7, 115
Megiddo 7
Melkart 119
merchant colony (Old Assyrian) 105
Merneptah (inscription) 115
Meshaʿ 99, 107
Stele/Inscription 51, 54, 56, 98–99, 121
Mesopotamia 67
Middle Ages 71
Miqne, Tel (Ekron) 8–9, 33
see also Ekron
Mizpah 11, 19
Moab 97, 99, 107, 121- 22
Moabite script 49
monasteries, Buddhist 105, 114 n. 1
Mudeni, Khirbet el- 120 n. 6

Naḥal Adorayim 10, 25 fig. 8
Naḥal Besor 25 fig. 8
Naḥal Gerar 25 fig. 8
Naḥal Guvrin 8, 10–11, 26, 32, 126
see also Beth Guvrin Valley
Naḥal HaElah 10–11, 11 n. 6, 25 fig. 8, 32
see also Valley of Elah, Elah Valley
Naḥal Lachish 8, 10–11, 18, 25 fig. 8, 26
see also Lachish
Naḥal Shiqma 10, 25 fig. 8
Naḥal Sorek 25 fig. 8
see also Sorek Valley
Ndembu 13, 15, 18 n. 11
Negev 31 n. 18
Nile River 124
Nimrud 36
Nineveh 36
Nippur 120
Nora 83
Stone/Inscription 55 fig. 4, 56, 77 fig. 5, 77

Old Aramaic, scripts/dialect 47, 65–66, 66 n. 8, 78
Old Byblian Script 52 fig. 3
Old Canaanite, scripts/epigraphic materials 45, 47–48, 50–51
Old Hebrew, script/alphabet 67, 73, 80–81, 83–84, 86–89
Old South Arabic 65–66
oral culture 61
Osorkon I 75–76

Padi 33
Panamu Inscription 78
periphery (vs. core) 12–13, 13 fig. 4, 16–17, 19
Philistia 7, 10, 14, 14 n. 7, 15, 17, 18 n. 11, 20–21, 26–28, 31–33, 35, 37, 119, 121–22, 124
Philistine Pentapolis 10, 25 fig. 8
Philistines 27–28, 31, 31 n. 18, 32–33, 36

Philistine script 49, 51
Phoenicia 10, 47, 73, 97, 107, 118–19, 124–25
royal inscriptions 74
Phoenician script 37, 47–48, 55, 70, 72–75, 77–83, 84 fig. 9, 84, 86–89, 119, 121, 123–24
early 84 fig. 9
lapidary scripts 55 fig. 4
linear 46, 48 n. 6, 49, 54
phonological isogloss(es) 65–66
pillar figurine(s) 34
Proto-Canaanite script 54
Proto-Hebrew 49
Pyrenees Mountains 17

Qubūr Walaydah bowl/inscription 49, 49 n. 9, 52

Raddana jar handle 49, 49 n. 9
Ramah 11, 19
Refaʿim Valley 25 fig. 8
Regal-ritual cities 12
Reḥov, Tel 2 fig. 1, 45 n. 1, 49, 49 n. 9, 83, 103
Revadim (ʾAbbaʿ) seal 49, 49 n. 10, 50, 52
Rite of Passage 13–14, 14 n. 7
rosette impressions 34
Roš Zayit, Khirbet 2 fig. 1, 81, 83
royal propaganda texts 122

Ṣafi, Tell eṣ- 1, 2 fig. 1, 11, 26, 31, 33
see also Gath
Samʾal 78
Samaria 2 fig. 1, 7, 25 fig. 8
inscribed ivories 120
Ostraca 98–99
Šamši-Adad 107
Sanskrit 105
Sardinia 55 fig. 4, 77, 83
Ṣārem, Tell eṣ- *see* Reḥov, Tel
Ṣareptah dipinto 48 n. 7
Sargon II 36–37
Script Dependent Hypothesis 69 n. 14
Sefire vassal treaty 108 n. 19
Semitic consonants 64 fig. 1
Sennacherib 10, 16 n. 8, 23, 31–33, 35–38
Seville Statuette 55 fig. 4, 77
shallow orthography 69, 69 n. 14
Shalmaneser III 107
Shephelah 4, 6–13, 15, 16 n. 8, 17, 18 n. 11, 19–21, 23, 23 n. 15, 25 fig. 8, 27–28, 30–35, 38, 45 n. 1, 119, 123
Sheshonk I 28, 30, 75–76
Shipiṭbaʿl 75–76, 98
Inscription 52 fig. 3, 75, 75 fig. 4, 80, 82, 87, 89
Shishak *see* Sheshonk I
Sidon 2 fig. 1, 77
Ṣidqa 34
Sinai Peninsula 11
sinnistrograde (script direction) 34
Socoh 25 fig. 8, 26, 32
Solomon(-ic) 100–2, 104, 121–26
Sorek Valley 8–9, 11 n. 6, 17–18, 23 n. 16, 26, 30–31, 31 n. 18, 32, 38
see also Vale of Sorek
South Asia 108 n. 18
South Canaanite script 46, 49, 53, 82–83, 86
see also inland script
Spain 17, 22 n. 14, 55 fig. 4, 77
St. Felix 16
stone weights 34
Šubʾil (seal) 66
Sudan 105
Syria 22 n. 14, 35 n. 20, 107

taršiš 83
taxation 100
Tel Dan Stele/Inscription 56, 99, 122
Tell Fakhariyeh 88
Statue Inscription 66 n. 8, 78, 84 fig. 9, 84–87, 88 n. 25, 119
Tell ʿOreme Inscription 120 n. 6

Tel Zayit Abecedary/Inscription
3 fig. 2, 3 n. 2, 12, 28, 37, 46 fig. 1, 47–54, 50 fig. 2, 52 fig. 3, 56, 62–63, 65–67, 71–72, 80, 81 fig. 8, 82, 82 nn. 23–24, 83, 85, 87–89, 97, 100, 102–4, 109, 113, 117, 122–26
Tel Zayit script 49
Timnah 8, 10, 23 n. 16, 25 fig. 8, 26, 32–35, 37–38, 81
see also Batash, Tel
Trans-Frontier Political Systems 15, 19, 25 fig. 8
Tret 16
Turkey 22 n. 14, 35 n. 20
Tyre 2 fig. 1, 77

Ugarit 99, 102, 104, 107, 115–17, 119
United Monarchy/Kingdom *see* Israel, United Monarchy
Uzziah 31–32, 36, 38

Vale of Sorek 8, 10, 32
see also Sorek Valley
Valley/Vale of Elah 26, 32
see also Elah Valley
Valley of Zephatha *see* Naḥal Guvrin
votive offerings 115, 117
votive texts 119

Wâdī el-Ḥesi *see* Naḥal Adorayim
Wâdī Selmān *see* Ayalon, Valley of
weights 106
Wenamun, Story of 118

Yeḥimilk 75–76
Inscription 52 fig. 3, 75, 82, 89, 118

Zakarbaʿl 47 n. 3
Zakkur Inscription 85 fig. 10, 89, 99
Zambia 13
Zayit, Tel 1, 1 n. 1, 2 fig. 1, 4, 6–8, 10–12, 15, 16 n. 8, 21, 23, 23 n.16, 24 fig. 7, 24–26, 25 fig. 8, 27 fig. 9, 28, 30–32, 34, 37, 45, 45 n. 1, 50, 54, 63, 71–72, 84, 102, 116, 118–19, 124–26
Zeitah Excavations 24 fig. 7, 27 fig. 9